First published in 2013 by Cool Springs Press, an imprint of the Quayside Publishing Group,
400 First Avenue North, Suite 400, Minneapolis, MN 55401

Cool Springs Press titles are also available at discounts in bulk quantity for industrial or sales-promotional use. For details write to Special Sales Manager at Cool Springs Press, 400 North First Avenue, Suite 400, Minneapolis, MN 55401 USA. To find out more about our books, visit us online at www.coolspringspress.com.

Library of Congress Cataloging-in-Publication Data

Fowler, Veronica Lorson.
 Backyard water gardens : how to build, plant & maintain ponds, streams & fountains / by Veronica Fowler.
    p. cm.
  Includes index.
  ISBN 978-1-59186-553-7 (softcover)
  1. Water gardens--Design and construction. I. Title.

 SB423.F67 2013
 635.9'674--dc23
                    2012044887

Acquisitions Editor: Billie Brownell
Design Manager: Cindy Samargia Laun
Designer: Wendy Holdman
Cover Designer: Connie Gabbart

Printed in China

10 9 8 7 6 5 4 3 2 1

Backyard
Water Gardens

HOW TO BUILD, PLANT & MAINTAIN PONDS, STREAMS & FOUNTAINS

VERONICA LORSON FOWLER

COOL
SPRINGS
PRESS
Growing Successful Gardeners™

MINNEAPOLIS, MINNESOTA

Acknowledgments

A special thank you goes to the staff at Aquascape, Inc., who contributed extensively to the creation of this book. Aquascape, a leading water gardening innovator and educator in North America, embraces a vision for water gardening that relies on a balanced ecosystem with the most natural balance possible of circulation, filtration, plants, fish, and rocks and gravel to ensure sustainability.

A special thank you goes to Marketing Communications Manager Jennifer Zuri as well as the several Aquascape staff experts who performed a technical review of this book: Ed Beaulieu, Dave Kelly, Brian Helfrich, and Gary Wittstock.

We are also indebted to the extensive use of Aquascape photography throughout this book. The Aquascape website provides an extensive source of the latest water gardening information and products, including a number of water gardening articles and how-to information. Visit it at **www.aquascapeinc.com**.

Photography and Image Credits

All photography and illustrations are courtesy of Aquascape, unless otherwise specified below.

Cover photo: GAP Photos/Elke Borkowski

Alpine Corp.: Page 36 (left)

Anita Nelson: Page 43 (bottom)

Beckett: Pages 35 (bottom left), 39 (top), 42 (top left and right), 58, 62, 65

BluWorld HOMElements: Page 36 (right)

Bond Mfgs: Page 37 (right)

Campania International: Page 37 (top and bottom)

Creative Publishing international: Pages 27, 91, 92, 95 (both), 96, 97, 99 (both), 100, 101 (both), 103 (both), 104 (both), 105, 108 (both), 109 (all), 115 (all), 119, 123 (all), 148, 153 (both), 154, 158, 164, 165 (both)

Jerry Pavia: Pages 18 (left), 43 (top), 141

John Meeks: Page 53

Joseph Tomocik: Page 135 (left)

Paula Biles: Pages 20 (top left), 34 (all), 41 (top), 42 (bottom), 135 (right)

Rosemary Kautzky: Pages 145, 147, 156

Backyard Water Gardens

The Pleasures of Water Gardening Across the Country

_W_ATER BRINGS ENTIRELY NEW LEVELS OF HOME AND BACKYARD enjoyment—the sound of splashing water; the color and movement of fish, exotic plants and flowers, and a sense of tranquility that is hard to find in any other way.

In a busy and often troubled world, something as simple as a backyard pond is a balm to the human spirit. And it's especially rewarding when you create this restful retreat yourself. It's amazing what you can do with some liner, a pump, maybe a filter, and a whole lot of stone.

Is it any wonder that water gardening is one of the most rapidly growing segments of landscaping and gardening across the country?

Regional Considerations

The severity or mildness of your winters is key in how you design, plant, and maintain your water feature.

Not surprisingly, how cold your winters get is a major factor in how you manage your water feature. In frost-free and very warm climates in roughly the lower third of the United States, primary concerns are keeping algae and potentially invasive plants in check during the colder times of the year.

Cold-Winter Water Features

If you live in a region that experiences freezing weather where the surface of the water feature will ice over, you will need to decide if you are going to continue to operate a waterfall or shut it down. Operating the waterfall during the winter will reward you with beautiful ice formations around the falls and stream beds. But you also have to consider that there will be a little maintenance required during this time of year, such as adding water due to evaporation and making sure ice dams don't form in the stream and waterfalls that could cause water loss over the edge of the stream.

As a result of the maintenance, many pond owners in cold climates simply choose to turn off the waterfalls during the winter. If you choose to turn off the waterfall, you will need to remove the pump from the filter and store it in a frost-free location, such as a garage or basement. If you have fish, then you will also want to consider

adding a floating de-icer. The de-icer will add the extra insurance that your finned aquatic friends will survive their winter slumber by making sure that there is always a hole open in the ice for oxygenation . . . even during extreme weather conditions.

Depth and size plays an important role in how winter-resistant your water garden is (see page 73). The deeper and larger the pond, the more stable the water temperature during the winter, resulting in less stress to the fish.

See page 158 for a complete listing of winter preparation chores.

Mild-Winter Water Features

Mild-climate gardens are those where the temperatures only occasionally go below freezing. If you live in this type of region, you are fortunate to be able to truly enjoy your water feature year-round. The water feature will still go through seasonal changes, just not as severe as the colder regions. Many of the aquatic perennial plants will go dormant during the cooler months, but will come back when the temperatures begin to rise. It is important during these cooler times of year, when the plants aren't helping filter and shade the water, to add beneficial bacteria to help balance the ecosystem and keep the algae under control.

A water garden in the North needs to be designed and maintained differently than one in the South.

National Zone Hardiness Map

You'll often hear gardeners refer to what "zones" a plant does well in. These usually refer to the U.S. Department of Agriculture (USDA) plant hardiness zones—regions designated by a number based on their average minimum winter temperatures.

USDA hardinesss zones are most useful to gardeners east of the Rockies, where broad expanses of states have similar growing conditions. They're less useful along the West Coast and mountainous regions, where there are many microclimates. Growing conditions in one microclimate can be very different from another microclimate just one mile away.

In the western part of the country, there have been efforts to create different zones based on average heat as well as average cold. Those are not referred to here.

The USDA Plant Hardiness Zone map was updated in 2012 to accommodate overall warming trends in some parts of the country in recent decades. So if your yard was in Zone 5 several years ago, it might well be redesignated as a Zone 6 now. Check the map to be sure.

Average Annual Extreme Minimum Temperature
1976–2005

Temp (F)	Zone	Temp (C)	Temp (F)	Zone	Temp (C)
-60 to -55	1a	-51.1 to -48.3	5 to 10	7b	-15 to -12.2
-55 to -50	1b	-48.3 to -45.6	10 to 15	8a	-12.2 to -9.4
-50 to -45	2a	-45.6 to -42.8	15 to 20	8b	-9.4 to -6.7
-45 to -40	2b	-42.8 to -40	20 to 25	9a	-6.7 to -3.9
-40 to -35	3a	-40 to -37.2	25 to 30	9b	-3.9 to -1.1
-35 to -30	3b	-37.2 to -34.4	30 to 35	10a	-1.1 to 1.7
-30 to -25	4a	-34.4 to -31.7	35 to 40	10b	1.7 to 4.4
-25 to -20	4b	-31.7 to -28.9	40 to 45	11a	4.4 to 7.2
-20 to -15	5a	-28.9 to -26.1	45 to 50	11b	7.2 to 10
-15 to -10	5b	-26.1 to -23.3	50 to 55	12a	10 to 12.8
-10 to -5	6a	-23.3 to -20.6	55 to 60	12b	12.8 to 15.6
-5 to 0	6b	-20.6 to -17.8	60 to 65	13a	15.6 to 18.3
0 to 5	7a	-17.8 to -15	65 to 70	13b	18.3 to 21.1

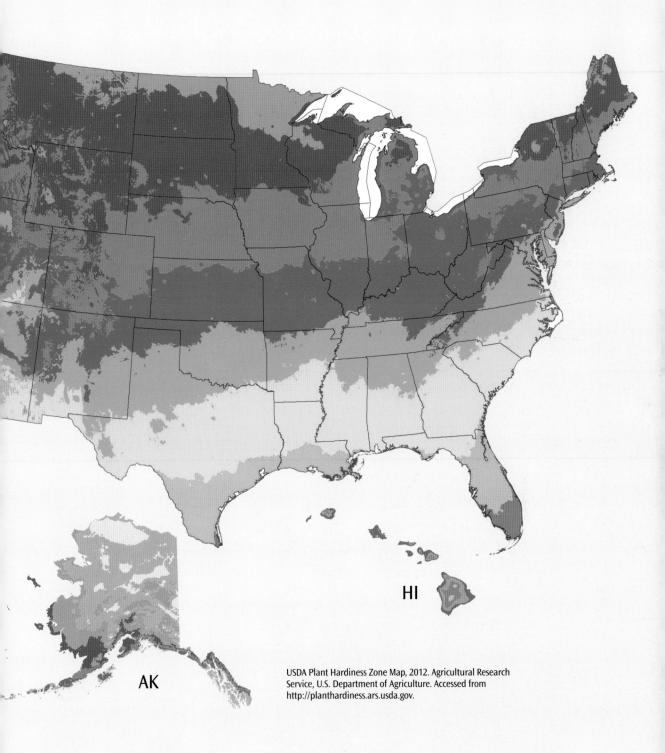

AK

HI

USDA Plant Hardiness Zone Map, 2012. Agricultural Research
Service, U.S. Department of Agriculture. Accessed from
http://planthardiness.ars.usda.gov.

ᚕ 1 ᚕ

Getting Started and Planning Your Water Garden

ADDING A WATER GARDEN IS A MAJOR UNDERTAKING, BUT IT MAY well be one of the best and most pleasurable garden additions you'll ever make. Take the time now—before you ever lift a spade—to thoughtfully design and plan your water garden. Doing your homework now saves frustrations and disappointment later. Learn about the best place to locate a water feature, the most fitting style, and the latest design and building techniques. The result will be a water feature that installs easily, requires minimal fuss, and is a focal point of your landscape for years to come.

What Kind of Water Feature Is Right For You?

Take a moment to decide the style and design of your water garden to fit your home, your tastes, and your lifestyle.

Choose a Style

Give some thought to the kind of personality you want your water garden to have. Ideally it should harmonize not only with your home's architecture, but also the character of the rest of your property.

It's equally important that your water garden match your lifestyle and your goals for it. Will it be a private retreat or a place to entertain guests? Will you enjoy it mainly during the day or evening? Do you have the time and desire to putter with extensive plantings and fish, or do you want something low-maintenance?

To arrive at a design, start with thinking about formal and informal styles, or create your own design that is a hybrid of the two.

Also draw inspiration from water gardens you've seen in person or in photos. Many approaches and styles have been used throughout history and still have an influence today—Moorish, Italian, French, Japanese, and others. Envision the flat, glassy planes of water at Tuscany's Villa Gamberaia. Or think of the lush natural look of Monet's water garden in France. Have fun and dream big dreams!

Formal Water Gardens

Formal water gardens are usually based on a symmetrical shape: a square, rectangle, or perfect circle or oval. Depending on how they're designed, they fit in with equally formal surroundings or a landscape that's quite informal.

A formal water garden can be a good choice for a smaller garden. Think of the little courtyards with fountains in Spain and Mexico. Large, expansive properties can also be compatible with a formal-style display.

With some formal water gardens, there is an emphasis on the reflections off the water surface. Many include a fountain or statuary. Formal pools and ponds also usually use regular, neat edging materials, such as bricks, blocks, and tiles. "Monoculture" plantings of just one plant, such as water lilies, are popular in formal water gardens. So are monochromatic planting schemes, using only white flowers, for instance.

Informal Water Gardens

Informal garden pools are more casual in shape and more versatile for planting schemes of all kinds. Pools in various irregular shapes, such as kidney, teardrop, lagoon, and "amoeba," are just a few of the ones you can either buy pre-formed or create with flexible line.

To give your informal garden that desirable "settled" look, take a cue from nature. Ponds in nature range from plants floating in deeper water, to plants growing in shallow water, to

This water garden is based on an abstract shape. Its natural stone edging and plantings give it a more casual feel.

plants growing on the banks. This transitional effect is easy to imitate. Place plants on your pool's side shelves (pre-formed liners often come with these shelves), or raise them up on a support. Then grow moisture-loving plants alongside your pool.

Go for a combination of plants that includes various colors, leaf forms, and textures. Water lilies and other aquatic plants that float or trail on the water's surface can be offset nicely by what professional landscape designers call "vertical accents" in the form of tall marginal plants. The combination lends your feature variety and interest.

Dimensions and Scale

The first rule of determining the size of your water garden is similar to criteria that landscapers use when designing a new flowerbed: It needs to be in scale.

That is, a water feature should neither be too big for its surroundings nor too tiny. If it is much too large, the water feature will overwhelm the area and look out of place. If it is too tiny, it will get lost in the crowd of other plants and other garden features, looking skimpy and undersized.

A Water Garden Is an Ecosystem

*The interplay of fish, plants, filtration, water aeration, and helpful bacteria
plays a critical role in maintaining a healthy water feature.*

A healthy water garden has clear water, active fish, and thriving plants. It smells and even feels in tip-top shape.

Fish do their part by eating mosquitoes and nibbling plants. Floating plants shade the water, preventing the growth of algae and keeping it cool and clear for fish. Marginal and submerged plants provide more cover for fish and other wildlife, and also filter impurities out of the water. A fountain aerates the water, keeping it oxygenated for fish. Filters catch particles in the water and prevent bacterial problems. A skimmer (see page 60) keeps debris off the surface of the water, and if you want, you can add filters inside the skimmer.

The Role of Bacteria

Every water garden needs different types of bacteria to keep the water healthy. Some bacteria foul the water, but others help keep it clear by breaking down debris and waste. One helpful type is nitrifying bacteria, which convert harmful ammonia from fish waste into less harmful nitrite and then nitrate—which is taken up in small quantities by plants as fertilizer.

The type of filter you choose (see page 59) can promote healthy bacterial growth. Some contain plastic balls, rocks, or media on which the bacteria are contained and continue to thrive.

The Role of Plants

Plants also play a vital role. Plant roots take up pollutants in the water, such as fish waste, use them as fuel for growth, then filter them and release oxygen into the water and air. Submerged plants are especially good at this because their many leaves are underwater, releasing oxygen directly into the water.

Floating plants are helpful too. They shade the water, greatly reducing the growth of algae, which needs sun to thrive. Floating plants also provide shade for fish so they don't overheat, and cover from overhead predators, such as birds or raccoons.

The Role of Pumps and Filters

In nature, water is filtered and aerated by running through layers of stone or moving along a streambed. In the artificial environment of a home garden, you must mimic this process with pumps and filters. These important pieces of equipment move water so that oxygen is incorporated into the water from the air. Well-oxygenated water prevents the growth of anaerobic bacteria, those bacteria that make stagnant water smell bad and feel slimy.

There are many different pumps and filters to choose from (see page 54), depending on the size of your water feature and the various options you desire. Even a tiny container garden

The Infinite and Constantly Revolving Ecosystem

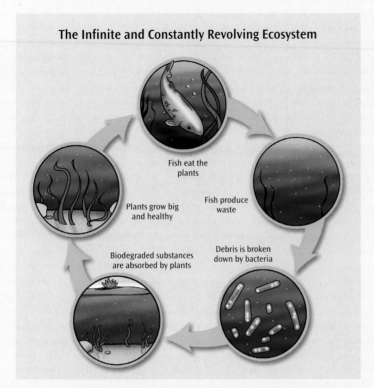

Fish eat the plants

Fish produce waste

Plants grow big and healthy

Debris is broken down by bacteria

Biodegraded substances are absorbed by plants

In order to have a successful water garden, you must understand the critical role of each component in a water garden and how they all complement one another.

does much better with a small pump and fountain to keep the water fresh. Smaller gardens need at least one good mechanical filter, while larger gardens need more complex filters and more powerful pumps to move the greater volume of water.

Mechanical filters must be rinsed every few days or so, especially in warmer weather. Still other filters contain beneficial bacteria and others zap organisms with UV rays.

The Role of Fish and Snails

Not every water feature needs fish, but they add a fascinating, beautiful element. The downside of fish is that they produce a lot of waste (think of that goldfish bowl you had as a kid). The waste then turns into ammonia, which can be toxic to the very fish producing it. Plants and filters are needed to remove these fish waste byproducts.

Fish eat mosquitoes and will graze on string algae. Snails eat algae along the sides of the pond.

The Role of Edging, Rocks, and Stones

Good edging keeps soil from silting into the pond, while rocks and stones provide tremendous surface area upon which beneficial bacteria thrive. The bacteria then break down excess nutrients in the water. Edging and stones also protect pond liners from UV light degradation.

Types of Water Features

Big or small? In-ground or above? Flexible liner or rigid? Do you want a waterfall? A stream?
Learn more about the different kinds of water features available to create one
that's just perfect for your landscape and your tastes.

If you are new to water gardening and just want to dip in your toes (so to speak), you may wish to start small, with a display that is more of a "garden accent." Or alternatively, you may have specific landscaping plans in mind and have no qualms about installing a substantial pool that will be the star of the show.

Following are the most common water feature options: fountains, container/tub, in-ground (you may use either a pre-formed shell or lay a special plastic sheet into a free-form shape), and aboveground. As desired, blend these with other features such as a fountain, waterfall, or streambed.

Fountains

There are so many choices in terms of fountain style, size, and sound that it's wise to do some serious preview shopping before you make your final decision. Water garden centers, home and garden centers, and mail-order suppliers offer an amazing range of options. For more stylish or customized fountains, search on the Internet for artists who specialize in such creations or prowl arts-and-crafts shows. With most fountains, the pump and tubing is built into the fountain, so you don't have to worry about those.

With wall fountains, match the material of the fountain with the wall or fence you'll be hanging it on. Go for compatible materials, and make sure you understand the manufacturer's recommended hanging methods before you buy. Otherwise, you may run into complications once you have it and try to mount it.

Container Water Gardens

Creative gardeners have come up with the most ingenious and charming little displays. You might want to try one as a garden accent (instead of or in addition to a more substantial water garden). Almost any watertight container can be used; even a small container garden can support plants. An umbrella stand, filled with

Fountains

Container water gardens

Rigid liner water gardens

Flexible liner water gardens

water, can host a taro, a papyrus, and/or a water-loving iris. A small bowl or kettle perched on a deck or patio can show off some duckweed, water lettuce, or a lovely mosaic plant (which displays small diamond-shaped leaves on the water's surface). If you want a fountain, you'll need to drill a hole in the bottom large enough to feed the plug through. Caulk around the hole to make it watertight. Or purchase a "spitter" or other ornamental water fountain, such as this bamboo fountain that rests right on top of a lined whiskey barrel. Larger water gardens can also support a few small fish as long as a fountain is included to keep water oxygenated.

Rigid Liner Water Gardens

Rigid liners are appealing because they take the guesswork out of digging and designing a water garden. They are usually made of strong, rigid black plastic or fiberglass. Designs include full or partial shelves on which to set plants as well as stream configurations or waterfall lips. Overall shapes include round, kidney-shaped, teardrop, and more. Rigid liners can measure up to 8 or more feet across.

The downside of rigid liners is that they are less forgiving than flexible liner and so are a bit trickier to install. Getting them perfectly level is a challenge, as is installing them in such a way that no uneven settling will occur. The edges of rigid liners also are problematic to conceal completely, if that's the look you want. This type of liner is resistant to leaks, but can indeed crack, especially in cold-weather areas.

Flexible Liner Water Gardens

Flexible liner is what the pros use, and for good reason. It can be used in just about any shape, and is fast and easy to install. It's also very forgiving in conforming almost perfectly to the shape of the hole you dig. While flexible liner can indeed be punctured, it's surprisingly tough. Flexible liner also works well with a variety of edging so that the liner is completely concealed by the edging and all you see is edging and water.

Aboveground Water Gardens

No digging required! Water gardens that are not sunken but rather sit on a surface—the ground, a patio, courtyard, terrace, or deck—are yet another option. (Just make sure the structure can bear the considerable weight and outward pressure of the water.) Larger than a container garden but smaller than most in-ground pools, aboveground water

Aboveground water gardens

Pools or ponds

features are increasingly popular. A raised pool is also a good option if your yard has heavy clay or rocky soil, any ground that would be difficult to dig in. Aboveground water gardens can use either flexible or rigid liners. Flexible liners must be attached to an outside, supporting structure, such as a wooden box.

Pools or Ponds

Highly formal or very natural looking, pools and ponds are simply any portion of a water garden that allows water to collect in a pool. They can be rigid liner or flexible, aboveground or below. Many pools are combined with waterfalls, streams, or different types of fountains.

Disappearing Small Water Features

These popular water features have a decorative element, such as stone or a vase, above the ground. Hidden underground is a reservoir topped with a grate and stone. Water is pumped up from the reservoir, spills over the decorative object, and then trickles through the stone back into the reservoir below. Think of it like a partly buried fountain.

Waterfalls

The charming splashing sound of a waterfall offers appeal for nearly any home. A waterfall can be a foot high or many feet high. It can be attached to a pool or pond or can be part of a stream. All waterfalls need pools at the bottom, but some have buried pools or reservoirs hidden from sight or have no visible pool or pond at all. Waterfalls can have one simple cascade or multiple cascades delivered from a hidden manifold, over multiple rocks or lips. Create your own waterfall with

Disappearing small water features

Waterfalls

Streams

stone or other materials, or use pre-formed weirs or waterfall forms. Waterfalls work with both rigid and flexible liners, depending on your design.

Streams

An artificial stream can be small, snaking just a few dozen feet. Or it can be huge, stretching for hundreds of yards. Streams are beautiful when they're worked into an existing slope, but they can also be created on flat landscapes. Most streams use segments of flexible liner, often overlapping and sealed with adhesive made just for that purpose. Larger stones along the edge anchor the liner, and smaller stones and gravel are spread out to conceal the liner for a more natural look. Most streams have at least a waterfall or two. Streams also can be part of a water garden design that includes one or more pools—or none. The water just constantly recirculates.

Pondless Waterfalls and Streams

The newest trend in water gardens is pondless waterfalls and streams. They can be large and spectacular—a real focal point for a backyard—but have almost no pooled water that would pose a threat for small children. An underground reservoir feeds the waterfall or stream, and an underground pool collects the water at the bottom, recirculating it once again. They have no fish and can be turned off at any time.

Pondless waterfalls and streams

The Anatomy of a Water Garden

Understanding how the various elements of a water garden interact is key to
creating a pool or pond that is easy to take care of and beautiful to behold.

Every water feature is as individual as the homeowner who builds it. But most larger water gardens share some key elements that keep them working harmoniously with clear water, healthy plants, and vigorous fish.

1 Skimmer-Pump-Filter

In this pond a combination skimmer-pump-filter continually pulls in water from the surface, filtering out debris such as floating leaves and algae. It then expels the filtered water through a hose, which is fed to the waterfall unit at the other end of the pond.

The filter in this setup is simply a "mechanical" filter, which removes particles from the water but does not biologically affect water clarity or other elements.

In other ponds, a pump might be encased in a different type of filter, or a filter might be attached to one end. The pump can then be connected with a hidden hose to a waterfall or a short fountainhead for a pretty spray effect.

This moving water also aerates the pond—essential for healthy fish, which die if they don't have enough oxygen in the water.

2 Liner

The liner is usually black and can be made from a flexible, waterproof plastic-like material or it can be rigid, almost like a child's wading pool.

3 Underlayment

Underlayment cushions the liner from both directions, preventing leaks from objects striking or pressing from above or sharp rocks or glass in the soil below.

4 Fish

Fish are more than just decorative. They also control mosquitoes by eating mosquito larvae.

5 Plants

Plants help shade the water to keep it cooler and clearer. They also are beautiful, adding greenery and sometimes flowers to your water garden.

6 Edging

This can be made of a variety of materials, but small boulders or flagstones are perhaps the most popular. They hold the liner in place, conceal it, and prevent soil and mulch from washing into the pond.

7 Shallow "Shelves"

These shelves, a few inches to several inches deep, are ideal for placing so-called marginal plants (bog plants) in pots. Marginal plants grow best in more shallow water.

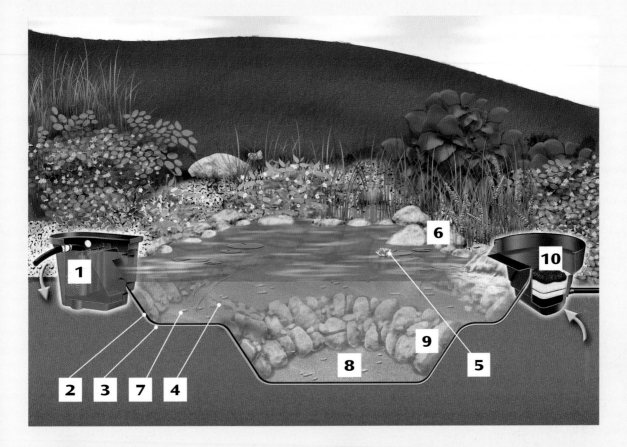

8 Deep Regions

Even in small ponds, deeper portions of the pond are less likely to freeze, creating a haven for fish during winter. Most deep regions of ponds are as shallow as 18 inches but seldom more than 3 feet deep. The deep regions are also where you place pots of those plants, such as water lilies, that like deeper water.

9 Rocks and Gravel

These disguise the liner for a more natural look, and also hold it into place.

10 Waterfalls/Biological Filter

There are different ways to create a waterfall in a pond, but this simple method simply takes in water pumped from the skimmer and pushes it over the lip of a premade waterfall unit—sometimes called a "weir"—for an attractive cascade.

This waterfall unit is also equipped with a "biological" filter; that is, the filter does more than just trap debris—it also deals with problem bacteria that can cause water to have a smell or to be discolored.

How Much Will Your Water Feature Cost?

Take a few moments to calculate how much your water feature project might cost.
This rough estimate of materials and supplies will help you scale your project
to your wallet so you can figure out how big to dream your dreams.

The cost of a water feature can vary tremendously. A small container water garden might cost under $50, while a large stream, waterfall, and pond can cost tens of thousands of dollars.

Below is a chart to help you create an approximate estimate of how much your water garden might cost. It does not include labor costs, which can be significant. One rule of thumb for figuring installation is to roughly double the cost of the material to calculate the cost of the labor. So $250 worth of stone, for example, will cost you about $500 to have it installed. A $200 pump/filter will cost about $400 for a contractor to install.

Once you have a specific design, it's smart to make a more specific budget so you know exactly the price tag your project is going to carry.

Calculating Water Garden Materials Costs

Small Water Features			
Container water garden with small pump	$50 and up		
Small freestanding decorative fountain	$100–$2,000		
Wall fountain	$150–$2,000		

Larger Water Features			
Materials	Small water garden of 8 feet by 6 feet with an average depth of 2 or so feet	Medium water garden with waterfall, large pondless waterfall, or a stream	Large water garden of 20 feet by 30 feet with an average depth of 2 feet with waterfall
Underlayment at about 40 cents per square foot	$30–$40	$150–$300	$350–$400
Liner at about $1.35 per square foot	$125 and up for flexible liner	$500 and up for flexible liner	$1200 and up
Pump	$50–$100	$200–$400	$400 and up
Filter	$75–$200	$100–$500	$400 and up
Tubing and fittings	$20–$50	$50–$200	$200 and up
Rentals	None	None	$400–$600 for a skid loader for one day
Stone, block, brick, etc. for edging (does not include stone used to create a waterfall or stream)	$50–$200	$200–$1,000	$500 and up
Electrical	$200–$400 for a licensed electrician to install a GFCI outlet, running from an existing GFCI outlet into your yard.		
Low-voltage lighting	$50–$150	$100–$250	$200–$600
Water garden plants	$20–$200	$20–$400	$200 and up
Fish	$10–$100	$50 and up	$100 and up

How Much Time Will Your Water Feature Take?

From a tiny container garden to an expansive pond with waterfall—the size and complexity of your water garden will dictate how much time it takes to build and maintain it.

Part of a rewarding water gardening experience is creating a water garden that you can manage easily with your limited time. Compared to flower beds, a water garden doesn't take a lot of time, but you do need to top off water levels, keep track of water clarity, clean out filters, tend to water garden plants, and troubleshoot.

To give you an idea of the time needed: A professional pond company, with all the right tools at the ready and experience on its side, can build a 150-square-foot pond in about 40 man hours.

Below is a chart that estimates how much is needed to create and maintain a water garden, from research right through maintenance, for years to come.

Be realistic in calculating how much time it will take to build your water feature so that you don't get frustrated or run into seasonal difficulties.

Estimated Time for Water Feature Building

Hours	Small water garden of 8 feet by 6 feet with an average depth of 2 or so feet	Medium water garden with waterfall, large pondless waterfall, or a stream	Large water garden of 20 feet by 30 feet with an average depth of 2 feet with waterfall
Researching (reading, online research, workshops, garden tours)	4–10 hours	6–12 hours	10–16 hours
Purchasing and assembling materials	2–4 hours	3–8 hours	8–plus hours
Digging	1 to 6 hours, depending on the soil	4–16 hours by hand	A day or two for a bobcat rental
Pump, filter, and tubing/ plumbing installation	Less than one hour	1–2 hours	2–4 hours
Installing liner and underlayment	less than hour for flexible liner; 1–2 for rigid	2–3 hours	2–3 hours with 2–3 people
Positioning stones, installing edging	2–4 hours	6–8 hours	1–3 days
Maintenance during spring, summer, and fall*	15–20 minutes week	1 hour a week	2 hours a week

* A few to several hours are needed in spring and fall for setup and cleanup.

Do It Yourself or Hire a Professional?

Once you decide the approximate size and type of your water garden,
determine if you can do it all yourself or if you need to bring in professional help.

Depending on the size or complexity of your water feature, you may well be able to do it all yourself. But with larger projects, it may be smart to hire a professional for at least a portion of the design and installation.

Designing

For a small project, designing it yourself is fine. For larger projects, you'll need to understand GPHs, flow rates, maximum head, amps, and watts. An experienced garden designer can review your plans and make recommendations, saving you headaches, redos, and having to purchase new expensive pumps or parts because you didn't calculate correctly the first time.

A fee for this type of consultation is usually small, and many designers do it for no charge in the hopes that you'll buy plants or other supplies from them.

Digging

Depending on the soil and the size of the project—not to mention your personal fitness level—you may be able to dig the water garden yourself. Or you may be wise to recruit friends and family to help. If you're not on a tight timeline, you can also dig the garden in short segments, stretched over a period of several days or more. You can also rent a small backhoe for larger projects, if you're comfortable operating one.

Remember that roots and rocks and clay soil can make digging difficult. Be practical about how much you can reasonably dig without straining your back. Also take into account where you'll put all that excavated soil. You may need to hire a contractor just to remove the soil.

Smaller digging projects can usually be handled on your own, especially if you recruit friends to help or spread the digging out over several days.

Stonework

Small simple water features seldom need professionals to assist with the stonework. But if you are dealing with larger boulders, you may need to hire strong workers who have specialized techniques for moving large stones, as well as their specialized equipment for moving them.

Pumps and Plumbing

With pumps and filters, the most difficult part is usually choosing the right type and size for your project. Installing them is usually fairly straightforward.

However, if you are getting into major plumbing, such as installing a water supply and cutting into the main water supply line, it might be best to hire a professional.

Electrical

As you can imagine with any project that combines water and electricity, it's critical to proceed with caution. If in doubt, hire a professional.

The first issue is calculating the additional power needed. When planning to install a powerful pump, check to see if your circuit box can handle the additional load. If you need to upgrade the box, that's a job for a professional.

The other issue is just flat-out safety. If you have any doubts about your ability to safely install, say, a GFCI outlet, turn to a certified electrician. It's also possible that it's not your decision. Some city codes mandate that certain electrical work be done by a certified electrician.

Codes may also specify rules that are dictated by local conditions in soil and climate, such as regulating how deep conduit must be buried. It may also specify what type of conduit is used.

Finding a Good Water Garden Contractor

- Find a contractor who specializes in water features, waterfalls, streams, aquatic plants, and fish as a primary business.
- Look at their portfolio or go out and visit their other jobs.
- Talk to the homeowners they've worked for. Otherwise, ask for references and follow up.
- Get it in writing. Contracts prevent misunderstandings and make it clear who will pay for what if something goes amiss. Also, whenever possible, get all changes and specifics in writing, even if it's just an email. Drawings are also helpful (keep a copy). Putting it on paper makes it clear and prevents confusion.

Plumbing for small- to medium-sized gardens is fairly simple. However, if your project is large enough that you might need to cut into the main water supply line, hire a pro.

Children and Water Features

Build it and they will come. Water attracts children like a magnet, so keep their safety in mind.

Even if you don't have children, chances are good that at some point or another, children will be around your water feature. Neighborhood kids will find it irresistible. Young visitors will naturally be drawn to it.

If you have children in your household or small children are frequent visitors, you'll need to think long and hard about what type of water feature to build and its overall safety.

The good news is that most backyard features are no more than 2 to 3 feet deep. The bad news is that with small children, it takes very little water to facilitate a tragedy.

No water garden is absolutely childproof. But there are tricks in designing and building water gardens—even large ones—that present less of a safety hazard for small children.

Check Out Ordinances and Laws

Depending on the size and depth of your pool, municipal ordinances or codes may require a fence around your yard or pool. Also review your homeowner's insurance to make sure it covers accidents related to a water feature on your property. If not, you should consult your insurance agent.

Depth

Pools and ponds may be shallow, but they eventually become covered in slick moss and algae, causing even adults to slip and fall. The safest choices are those features with no pooling, such as pondless waterfalls or recirculating fountains or millstones surrounded by stone.

Edging

What surrounds your water feature also is important. A fountain or aboveground water feature just a foot or so high can be dangerous for toddlers who can tip forward into them. Broad, flat edging, such as wood planks or cut stone, invites children to walk on top of it like a path.

The safest edging for children is that which gradually gets deeper since it's more difficult for them to plunge into the water feature rapidly.

"Pondless" waterfalls are increasingly in demand because they offer the beauty and sound of a water feature without the pools of water than can harm children. Water flows into a reservoir under the rock, and then is recirculated to the top of the waterfall.

Placement

Whenever possible, position a water feature where you can see it from the house. Not only will you be able to keep an eye out for children, but you'll also be able to enjoy your water feature more.

If you are building an in-ground pool into a deck or off the side of a deck, consider railing or other barriers to prevent both children and adults who might not be paying attention from falling in.

Children are likely to wade into water if they can, so design edging with that in mind. And never leave children unsupervised around a water feature. Even when it's shallow, stones become slippery with moss and algae.

Building the Child-Proof Water Garden

Children can come to harm in water gardens, and they can also harm water gardens.

Children can't help but be inquisitive and experimenters. They like to rearrange and pick up stones, spill chocolate milk into ponds, pour bubble soap into water, poke sharp sticks into liners, pull out marginal plants, harass fish, and more. They love to walk on carefully laid edging, often damaging or dislodging stones.

If you have children or grandchildren, you'll simply have to teach them to "look, not touch" the water garden—no leaning over to dip fingers in it or touch it or walk around it without supervision.

That said, it's best to design the most indestructible water garden possible. Don't invest in expensive fish. Keep delicate sculptures for another part of the garden (or in the house). As much as possible, place loose rocks into cement or waterfall foam to prevent pint-sized visitors from rearranging them.

Siting Your Water Feature

Just as with installing a new flower garden or planting a new shrub or tree, it is critical to select an appropriate location for your water feature. A good site sets you up for easy care, maximum enjoyment, and minimal expense and hassles.

Site Features to Seek Out

Plentiful sun. The majority of water plants adore full sun and bloom with gusto as a result—specifically, at least six hours per day. A spot that is suitable for a flowerbed or vegetable garden can easily host a water garden.

That said, especially in the southern half of the United States, some shade *can* be good, especially in the afternoon. Light shade is particularly helpful for smaller ponds, because the water heats up easily.

An open setting. Choose a spot away from large trees and shrubs, which interfere from below with roots and from above with falling leaves and twigs.

The best spot for a water feature also has ample elbow room. You will be able to tend your water garden more readily and admire it more easily. Sufficient air circulation is also good for the health of the plants—and the fish.

A level surface. This is important because water always responds to gravity and for best visual effect and best water flow, you need to get edges perfectly level. Granted, few sites are naturally completely level, but don't worry about minor changes in grade—it's easy to make the necessary minor adjustments during installation.

Good visibility. You will enjoy your water garden so much more, potentially at all times of the day and all seasons of the year, if you can view it easily from your house and/or patio or deck. Being able to see it well is also a safety issue, just in case someone or something falls in.

An easy way to mark out your future water feature is to use spray paint to outline the shape on the grass.

While most water gardens are in the backyard where owners can enjoy them with more privacy, a water garden right by the front porch offers a soothing welcome and a relaxing spot for sharing a chat or cold beverage with a visiting friend.

An electrical source. The ideal site for a water feature that will use electricity (a pump, fountain, or filter, for instance) is near an outdoor power outlet.

If there isn't an outlet close to the site you want, you or an electrician can run a freestanding outlet to the area.

All outdoor wiring needs to be protected by a GFCI or GFI (ground fault circuit interrupter or ground fault interrupter), a type of electrical outlet that automatically shuts off power when it detects a problem with the circuit, thus preventing shock.

Site Features to Avoid

Low-lying spots. In nature, ponds are often located in low-lying places where water naturally collects. However, in an artificial water feature, too much natural water from rain or runoff might overflow your pond and affect water quality on a regular basis. Or water from below can create pockets of trapped water that create bubbles in the liner.

If your yard has a swampy, low-lying area, consider turning it into a bog garden rather than a water feature with a liner. Bog gardens are filled with moisture-loving plants and often have standing water.

Steep slopes. A pool or pond really doesn't belong on a slope or hillside. It can be done, with a lot of shoring up and the inclusion of diversion channels so unwanted water doesn't flow in. But the weight may cause your efforts to backslide or slump after a while.

Streams and waterfalls are another issue. They can be gorgeous on sloping land, but take into consideration the additional pump power needed to move all that water upwards.

Underground lines, pipes, and cables. Do not plan a water garden in an area where there are— or might be—underground cables, pipes, sewer lines, or a septic field. These can be obstructions or worse, safety hazards. Further, your display could potentially block access to them. Before deciding on your water garden site, call your utility company or city or county government to have a trained professional come out and check. This service is usually free.

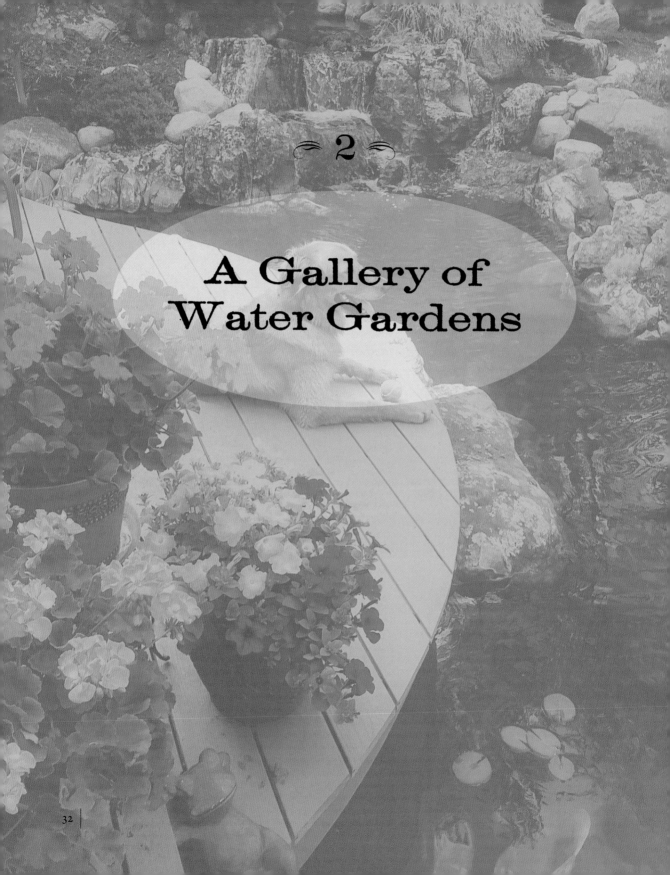

≈ 2 ≈

A Gallery of Water Gardens

*I*N THIS CHAPTER, WE'LL LOOK AT THE VARIOUS SORTS OF WATER gardens you can install, from a charming container tucked into a nook to spectacular combination stream-waterfalls-ponds that sprawls across a huge backyard.

Water gardening is more varied than ever and the choices are amazing. Fountains, statuary, lighting, formal pools, natural ponds, and many other inspiring water features are highlighted in these pages. Flip through this chapter to get a clearer picture of what water garden is right for you, your home, and your lifestyle.

Container Water Gardens

Some of the smallest water gardens are also the most striking. Check out this gallery for ideas and inspiration. Simply start with a container, add water, plants, and perhaps a pump. You'll have a water garden that is small on size, but big on style.

Just as you would stage pots filled with flowers, arrange pots filled with water garden plants. Make ordinary pots waterproof by inserting black plastic pot-like tubs inside the pots. Nest pots of water garden plants inside the tubs, and then fill the tubs with water.

With an oversized urn as beautiful as this one, nothing more is needed than water. If a pot has a drainage hole in it, just block the hole with waterproof exterior caulk.

One-of-a-kind finds from flea markets, specialty garden shops, or travels can be turned into beautiful water gardens. This exquisite stone head, topped with a stone bowl, is put to unusual use by filling it with water and floating a few water hyacinths on top.

This large water dish garden is simplicity itself. Marginal plants thrive in pots set inside the waterproof dish. Water lettuce floats on top and a water lily, also growing in a pot set inside the dish, is happy enough in its home to send out pink flowers.

The number of pre-made container water gardens now available is astounding. This series of container water gardens is as much a fountain as it is a water garden. Each urn is interconnected and refills the other. It plugs into a nearby outdoor outlet.

Show off your personality by creating a container garden that matches your personal style. This pink, mirrored pot was turned into a container garden in minutes by outfitting it with a 70-gph pump made especially for small container gardens. Secure in place with decorative stones, fill with water, and you're done!

Fountains

Among the simplest of water gardens, fountains are usually ready-made features that are freestanding or attach to a wall or fence.

The classic shape of this fountain is designed to do double duty as both a fountain and a birdbath. Birds can't resist the sound of splashing water!

Freestanding fountains such as this one are gorgeous to stand up to let light sparkle through the water or to set against a wall, indoors or out. It's made of metal and glass, so it's heavy enough to resist light winds but should not be set where stronger winds might topple it. Position so the power cord is hidden. In this case, a hole was drilled through the deck and the cord runs under the deck to a GFCI outlet.
Photo: Bluworld HOMelement

Hanging fountains should be of a material and style that works with the wall behind them. This classic traditional fountain, made of resin and fiberglass, is a perfect accent to a stone wall, but it would also look good on stucco or brick. It's also light enough to make hanging easy. It's a recirculating fountain, so all you need to do is hang, add water, and plug in. (Conceal the electrical cord by drilling a hole and running it behind or through the wall. Or hide behind electrical raceway or foliage.) Photo: Campania International

This self-contained fountain is made of a stone resin realistic enough that it can take two people to move it, even without water. Lights are embedded in the bottom basin so you can enjoy this fountain 24 hours a day. Photo: Bond Manufacturing

Floor fountains are an easy, instant option. This quality version is made of cast stone, so it's very heavy and durable. The cord can be hidden under soil, gravel, or foliage. Photo: Campania International

Disappearing Fountains

A little bit magical, "disappearing" fountains sit atop underground reservoirs that recirculate the water.

This classic, blue urn-like fountain comes as a complete kit, including a reservoir with a slatted cover onto which the urn snugly attaches.

Stones don't always need to be stacked. This kit uses a basalt stone column, predrilled vertically, and sold with pump, reservoir, and other components. (See page 67 for a cross-section of this fountain.) But, you could have a stone drilled yourself to create something similar. Or prep several stones for multiple fountains, each with flexible tubing running from its base onto a manifold attached to a single pump.

This ceramic urn is also part of a kit, but you could use any pretty glazed ceramic pot or vase and make something similar yourself.

This bowl fountain is created from a kit that comes complete with tubing, a pump, and an underground reservoir with a plastic grate. Water spills over the lip of the bowl into the hidden reservoir and then a pump propels water upward to flow down and recirculate all over again.

This cross-section illustration shows how simple seemingly mysterious disappearing fountains are. Make them with a kit like this one, or design your own starting with a 5-gallon bucket or larger container sunk into the ground. Just make sure the container is weather resistant so it won't crack or leak. The electrical outlet must be protected with a Ground Fault Circuit Interrupter.

In-Ground Pools and Ponds

Pools dug out of the ground are easy to make, highly functional, and practical.
The surrounding soil insulates the water features for more stable water temperatures.

This formal water feature is sunk into the ground and surrounded with brick edging, mortared into concrete. The urn-style fountain is an elegant touch that also aerates the water.

Even in a small backyard, an in-ground pool (with a waterfall built up with stone) creates a pleasant retreat.

Built into the patio, this pool is serenely elegant with a formal shape and thin stone pavers stretching uninterrupted to the edge. The simple in-pond fountain is powered by an electrical line installed when the patio was built, running underneath the pavers.

With in-ground features, you can position them so they're below the viewing area, allowing you to take in the whole scope of the waterscape.

Aboveground Water Features

If you have problem soil, want to put a water feature on top of a hard, paved surface, or simply enjoy the look of an aboveground pool or pond, the possibilities are endless.

This striking combination fountain-pool was made with a special kit. Just add your own bricks, stones, or pavers.

Well-chosen aboveground water features are striking when placed on top of a patio or deck, blending in perfectly and becoming part of the architecture.

This formal water garden is made with stacked stones and lined with flexible liner that fits neatly underneath the edging.

Flexible liner also is good to use with wood-sided raised water gardens. Raised water gardens also have the advantage of being easier to work in, making raising and lowering plants and other water garden chores gentler on the back and providing more sure footing.

Waterfalls

*Small or spectacular, high or low, broad or narrow, waterfalls never cease to amaze.
They add a special sound to a water garden that can't be replicated in any other way.*

For a truly natural look, incorporate fallen logs into the stonework of a waterfall or stream. Wood doesn't last as long as stone, but in most cases will last 10 or more years and can then be replaced.

One of the easiest waterfalls to build is simply to install a pre-formed plastic waterfall reservoir topped with a lightweight artificial stone made specifically for the task. Surround it with natural stone.

For this waterfall seeping out of a cut-stone wall, a wide and small pool was constructed behind the wall. Liner runs from the pool, all the way downward behind the wall, and continues into a small pool and stream at the foot of the falls.

Waterfalls don't need to be large. This waterfall uses a pre-formed plastic waterfall reservoir. Stones have been secured with special waterfall foam (a type of adhesive) right on top of the lip. The effect is more like water bubbling across the stones rather than off them. Strategically placed plantings disguise the reservoir.

"Pondless" waterfalls without any pool above or at the foot are very popular. They're a wonderful addition to a landscape where children play or pets might plunge in. Water flows from the falls, down into an underground reservoir at the base, then is pumped up through flexible tubing to the top, where it is recirculated and flows back down all over again.

Waterfalls don't always need to be high and narrow. This broad waterfall cascades over a few wide, flat stones and into a pool.

The shape and placement of stone is key in creating different styles of cascades in waterfalls. Here, water sheets from a flat, thin stone that extends out farther than the others for a long, slender fall. Other cascades are created by water flowing off to the side and down almost a stairstep of stones.

Streams

Whether it's large and snakes across your entire property or small and snakes around nothing more than your patio, a stream is a wonderful way to draw the eye through a landscape with a splash of water.

Flat landscapes can have streams too. This stream was built with many stones to give height to the upper part of the stream. It then flows down into a pond, a beautiful feature to create at the head or foot of a stream.

Unlike many other water features, streams are well suited to natural wooded areas. Their moving water helps push away leaves and debris. And since they're shallow, working around roots is easier to cope with.

Even in a suburban backyard, a stream can fit in beautifully, stretching across a large lot and adding a natural element to what might otherwise be lost space.

With any water feature, it's important that you have a good place from which to view your handiwork. This gazebo is a delightful place to enjoy the sounds and sights of this stream.

3

Understanding Water Garden Components

IF YOU'RE NEW TO WATER GARDENING, THE DIFFERENT PARTS and elements of a water garden—all of which interrelate—can be bewildering. How deep and big should you make your water garden? Which pump to choose and how powerful should it be? How much will it cost?

In the following pages, you'll find out about all the different components and how they work. It's one of the great challenges—and pleasures—of water gardening: Learning to make all the components work together so well that you're almost not aware of them. Instead, they work behind the scenes to create a beautiful setting of clear splashing water, serene water lilies, and fish glinting in the sunlight.

Understanding Liners

Choosing a liner is one of the first major decisions you'll have in designing a water garden.
Rigid or flexible?

Pre-formed Rigid Liners

Rigid liners are highly popular and can last a long time (though not forever). It is wise to invest in quality materials in order to get maximum mileage.

In particular, seek out good UV resistance because exposure to sunlight weakens plastic and causes it to crack and leak over time.

When shopping for a pre-formed pool liner, you will find plenty of choices. They tend to be strong, rigid black plastic or, less commonly, fiberglass. You may see ones with full or partial shelves, ones with stream configurations or waterfall lips, round ones, kidney-shaped ones,

teardrops, and so on. They can be 2, 3, or even 5 feet across and 6 feet long or longer.

Prices vary widely. Fiberglass is more expensive (perhaps $400 for a 6-foot by 3-foot pool compared to just $200 for plastic) but lasts longer—up to 50 years—and is more resistant to cracks from settling and from frost and thaw cycles in cold climates.

It would seem that installing a rigid liner would be easier than a flexible liner. However, especially if you have a complex shape with multiple levels, it can be difficult to dig the hole to conform perfectly. It's important to dig away as little soil as possible so there's a minimum of settling

A flexible liner conforms to just about any shape and its edges are easy to conceal.

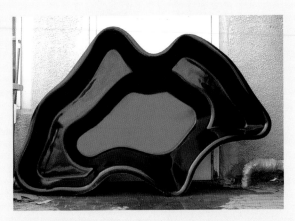

A rigid liner takes the guesswork out of water garden design.

once the liner is in position. You must also backfill in very precisely to support marginal shelves and the weight of the water. Otherwise, settling—a common problem with rigid liners—may occur.

With all liners, it's important to get the liner level, but this is especially true with rigid liner. If the rigid liner isn't perfectly level, it will be very apparent since the water will slope unevenly from one side to the other.

Flexible Liners

Flexible liners allow you to create a pond or stream of just about any size or shape. It's easier to completely conceal flexible liners than it is rigid liners because you can wrap and shape edges precisely the way you want to work with the edging you choose.

Choose liner made specifically for ponds. They hold up to the special conditions of a water garden, including UV light, and are fish-safe.

Professional water garden designers recommend the three following types of flexible liner, purchased separately or as part of a kit.

45-mil EPDM rubber

EPDM stands for ethylene propylene diene monomer. Considered the liner of choice for most jobs, it is extremely durable and puncture-resistant. It's also extremely flexible, which is handy when trying to tuck and turn and twist liner into irregular shapes. This is especially important in a small pond, where you'll have to tuck and fold the liner a lot to fit into the small hole.

However, size is a limitation if you are doing a very large job. The largest roll size manufactured is 50 feet by 100 feet, and seaming two pieces of EPDM rubber is tricky. It is done on the site where you're installing your pond and requires the right temperature and humidity levels, a flat solid foundation to work on, and messy seam tape.

40-mil polypropylene

If your pond requires a liner larger than the 50 feet by 100 feet available for EPDM rubber, consider 40-mil polypropylene. It's actually more durable and puncture-resistant than 45-mil EPDM, but it's not nearly as flexible, so it's harder to conform to various holes and shapes.

30-mil polyethylene

Least expensive of liners, it costs about half of polypropylene and EPDM rubber. It's stiff and can be difficult to work with. It does not hold up well to the beating it takes from the placement of large stone, so you must be especially careful with it. And for large projects, it can't be seamed without expensive welding equipment, usually by a professional.

Understanding Pumps

If you're good at math, you may enjoy figuring out what kind of pump to get.
If you're not, well, do some rough calculations and then check with a water garden
professional to help you make the final choice.

Pumps are critical to a successful water garden. They power waterfalls, pull water through filters, and spray water from fountains.

Pumps come in a variety of sizes and styles, and can be combined with other features of a water garden. A small pump for a container water garden may have a filter and fountainhead built right in. Another medium-sized pump may have a foam-type filter attached, or should be placed in a filter box.

Adequate power is key. Too little power and the pump creates a weak, unappealing waterfall or fountain, or hinders filters and skimmers from working well.

With pumps, you get what you pay for: durability and power. The smallest pumps start at around $20 for tabletop versions. A pump large enough to power a nice bubbler fountainhead in a pool maybe the size of a large bathtub costs about $80.

And a pump that will turn over the volume of a medium-sized pond, power a fountainhead, a pressure-fed filter, *and* a waterfall 2 or 3 feet high might cost $175 or so.

The key number to know in choosing a pump is gallons per hour. You need a pump powerful enough to turn over the entire volume of your pond, stream, or waterfall at least once every hour. So a 300-gallon pond needs a 300 or more GPH pump.

When in doubt, buy a more powerful pump (perhaps 25 to 50 percent more than you think you need). You can restrict the flow—most pumps have valves to adjust this—but you can't add power needs.

GPH needs can be surprisingly high. If you are building an 8-foot by 4-foot pond, 2 feet deep, with a 15-foot stream attached, topped by a waterfall that rises 2 feet, you will need a pump with a 1,200-1,500 GPH. (Price: anywhere from $70 to $500.)

This type of pump is perfect for a container or tub garden or to run a small statuary fountain. Water is taken into the strainer at the bottom side and into the pump. It's propelled up the tube through the top, into a fountainhead, statue-type fountain, or a small hose (for a small waterfall). Note the small knob that allows you to control the force of the pump.

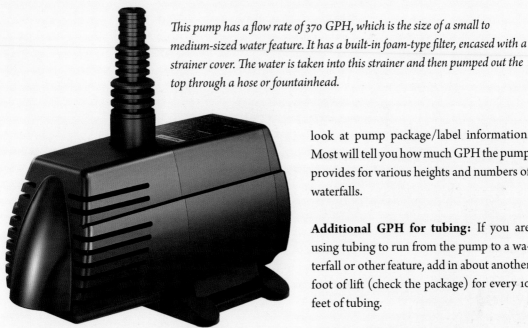

This pump has a flow rate of 370 GPH, which is the size of a small to medium-sized water feature. It has a built-in foam-type filter, encased with a strainer cover. The water is taken into this strainer and then pumped out the top through a hose or fountainhead.

look at pump package/label information. Most will tell you how much GPH the pump provides for various heights and numbers of waterfalls.

Additional GPH for tubing: If you are using tubing to run from the pump to a waterfall or other feature, add in about another foot of lift (check the package) for every 10 feet of tubing.

Additional GPH for a more generous flow of water over falls, especially wide waterfalls: Use this rough rule of thumb—for a 1-inch thick sheet of water 1 inch wide over a waterfall, add 150 GPH to the pump. For 1 inch of water flowing 6 inches across, add 900 GPH.

Additional GPH for waterfalls: Besides the number of gallons in your water feature, you also need to know how much additional GPH your pump will need to achieve lift for any waterfall. The easiest way to determine this is to

How to Calculate GPH

Water gardens are seldom neat, regular, geometric shapes that make it easy to calculate the overall volume of the water. So figuring out the volume—and therefore determining a key number in choosing a pump—is tricky.

You can do some general estimating by taking simple measurements. With a pond that is a roughly oval abstract shape, measure how long it is, how wide, and how deep in the deepest part and then calculate it the same way you would a rectangular box. You can also figure out how wide, on average, a stream is and how deep it will be.

Then calculate the number of cubic feet of water. Convert cubic feet into gallons by multiplying by 7.48.

This method give you more gallons than the actual amount, but within reason that's okay because your pump should be powerful enough to turn over *at least* the total volume of water every hour.

There are several helpful online calculators for figuring out how many gallons of water your water feature will contain and the GPH needed.

Typical Parts of a Pump

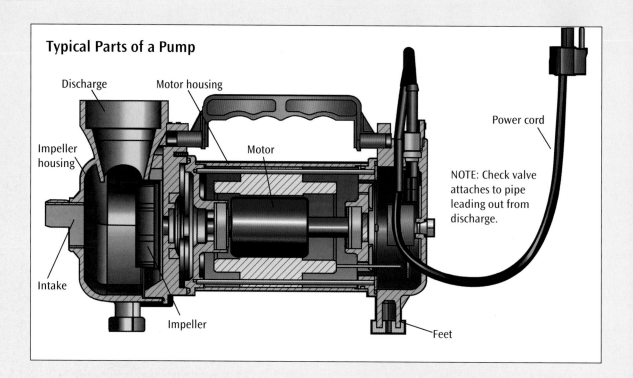

Discharge

Motor housing

Power cord

Impeller housing

Motor

NOTE: Check valve attaches to pipe leading out from discharge.

Intake

Impeller

Feet

Smart Shopping

If even thinking about GPH makes your head spin, rely on the experts. Go pre-shopping online, at a home-improvement store, or a store specializing in water features. Talk to the most knowledgeable person available. Also look at the box or label on the pump. It will have a lot of detailed information in chart form.

Other questions to ask:

- How long is the cord? It should be long enough to reach your electrical source. You should be sure to use an outdoor-rated extension cord. Otherwise, you will have to purchase materials to splice on additional cord.
- How much will the electricity cost? Check with your local utility to see how much you pay per

kilowatt. Then use this formula: Watts x 24 hours (in a day) × 30 days (in a month) divided by 1,000 = number of kilowatts per month × cost per kilowatt = total monthly cost of operating a pump.

An experienced water garden contractor also can tell you approximately how much you should expect to pay per month in electricity.

- What is the warranty? Most pumps are guaranteed for at least one year.
- Ask about return policies. If your pump doesn't do the job, can you return it?

Additional GPH for fountains: Check the package on the filter or fountain itself. It should list the additional GPH needed. A small splashing statuary, for example, requires 50 to 150 GPH.

Additional GPH for filters: If a filter is powered by gravity, such as a skimmer filter where the water just flows in it, you won't need additional GPH. But if the pump is needed to propel water through the filter, additional GPH is required. If the filter is not built into the pump, the file or product information should specify how much additional GPH is needed.

Let the Experts Do the Work

If all the calculations involved in a water garden give you a headache, here's an easy solution: Buy a kit. The manufacturer has done all the calculations and figured out the details for you.

Look for a kit designed for the size and style of water feature you want. Home centers carry an increasing variety, but water garden specialty stores and online sources have far greater inventory so that you can locate just the right kit for you.

A Water Garden Pump Glossary

Amps and watts: Refers to the amount of electricity used by the pump. It gives you an idea of how powerful it is and also helps you figure out how much it will cost to run—which can be surprisingly expensive in some cases.

GPH: Gallons per hour. Determines how much water the pump can move per hour.

Head and lift: Two very similar but slightly different terms. Head is the amount of force that a pump can force through tubing and other spaces. Lift is how *high* the pump can force the water (lift, therefore, includes gravity). The combined value of head and lift will give you the "total dynamic head"—the number that will tell you the amount of water produced at a given lift and distance from the pump to the discharge location.

Magnetic-driven/direct-driven: Direct-driven pumps, also called induced pumps, use more electricity but are less expensive to purchase.

They also have better lift to power waterfalls and other features.

Magnetic-driven pumps use less electricity but are more expensive. However, if you will be using a considerable amount of electricity to power your water feature, it may pay off in the long run.

Maximum head and maximum lift: This is the amount of force or height a pump could force water if there were absolutely no restrictions, such as friction from tubing or gravity, against it.

Submersible/nonsubmersible: A submersible pump, the kind you set in the water, should be sufficient for nearly any DIY water garden project. Nonsubmersible pumps, the kind that are installed outside the water, are extremely powerful (5,000 GPH or more) and usually needed for only the most spectacular home or commercial displays.

Understanding and Choosing Filters

The function of a filter is simple: to filter the water to keep it clear and free of debris.

But choosing a filter is a little more complicated. There are a number of different filters out there, and depending on the size of your water garden and how clear you want the water to be, you may need two or more different types of filters to achieve crystal-clear water that's never green.

Some pumps come with filters attached. Some pumps require a filter purchased separately. And pumps in tabletop or fountain water features usually have no filter at all since there won't likely be fish, plants, or other matter that will produce debris or waste. In fact, the more fish you have, the more heavy-duty your filtration needs. Just like in an aquarium, fish produce an enormous amount of waste that pollutes the water if it isn't naturally or artificially filtered out.

Mechanical Filters

A mechanical filter is basically a very good strainer. Water runs through it, pushed or pulled by a pump. Foam, netting, grates, or screening catches particles in the water.

Mechanical filters need regular rinsing out, usually every few to several days. This usually consists of lifting out the filter and giving it a hard spray with a hose for a minute or two.

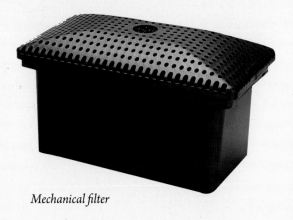

Mechanical filter

Prefilters

A prefilter is simply a type of filter that prevents particles from clogging a pump right before they are sucked into the pump.

Prefilters come in several different styles, such as a piece of foam that fits on the end of or around a portion of the pump or a removable device encased in plastic attached with a slatted snap-on encasement. Or the prefilter can be a separate mechanism alongside the pump, attached with tubing.

Shown here is a prefilter being removed from a combination pump-filter for a good rinse—much needed!

Biological Filters

A biological filter is basically a housing that provides the necessary habitat for beneficial bacterial colonization.

Like mechanical filters, biological filters come in many different styles. Most, however consist of a media of plastic, rock, or ceramic on which helpful bacteria live. Biological filters may also contain enzymes.

The water is pulled or pushed through the biological filter usually with the help of a pump. The water flows into the filter, over the media and the beneficial bacteria, and then back out into the pond. The water must be pumped constantly or the helpful bacteria can die. As with mechanical filters, you must clean biological filters occasionally—anywhere from every month or so to once a year. Shown at right is a bag of biomedia balls, which rest in a biofalls setup, getting a good hosing down.

Biological filter

Prefilter

UV Filters or Clarifiers

These expose water to ultraviolet light to kill problem-causing single-celled organisms, such as algae, fish parasites, and nonbeneficial bacteria. Water is pulled or pushed with a pump into a container equipped with an ultraviolet light bulb. The organisms that pass through and are pumped out with the water are exposed to the UV light, their DNA is altered, and they eventually die. It's an effective method for controlling floating algae.

UV clarifiers are discouraged by some water gardening professionals. They would rather see gardeners making sure their garden is in ecological balance and avoid UV clarifiers because they disagree with the assertion that the UV rays don't also kill beneficial bacteria and microorganisms along with the bad.

UV clarifiers are available housed in tube-like casing, or they can be a part of other types of filters in boxes. Still others are designed for mounting outside the pond. The one shown here is designed to be buried almost up to its top alongside the pond with water flowing through tubing connected to a pump.

UV filter or clarifier

Skimmer

Skimmer

This is basically a large box with an opening on the top of one side, positioned just below the surface of the water, off to one side of the water feature. Floating debris such as leaves and sticks flow into an inlet that looks like a window, level with water surface. The water flows into a box or net that catches leaves, twigs, debris, dust, pollen, and more and then is pumped out back into the pond. The skimmer box or net must be emptied periodically, depending on the site, the feature, and the time of year.

Skimmers are almost essential with large streams, since the stream and any waterfalls are open to a large area and therefore can catch a large amount of debris. Also, if the pump in a stream or waterfall gets clogged, it can stop the whole water feature from functioning. A skimmer prevents this.

Biofalls

Biofalls

The large pre-formed black plastic waterfall lips—also called weirs or header pools—often also contain some form of filtration. These filters may include sheets of foam, mesh bags of lava rock or bioballs, or other combination mechanical/biological filters. Some water gardeners even report success using special barley treatments in biofalls. Like all filters, biofalls must be cleaned out from time to time. Most need to be cleaned once a year.

The pre-formed waterfall here usually has media, such as a bag of bioballs, or foam-type filter mats to filter the water that flows through from the bottom and up over the top of the lip.

Fountainheads and Ornaments

What a delightful way to add movement, sparkle, and splash to your pond or pool!

A fountainhead is an easy, inexpensive way to create splashing water in your pool or pond. Widely available in most do-it-yourself stores and elsewhere, it's usually attached to a pump with a piece of pipe that comes with them or is sold separately.

Fountainheads are more than just pretty. They help aerate the water, keeping it oxygenated for fish.

Choose from a variety of fountainhead styles. Shown here are three of the most popular, but there are dozens of different patterns available.

Often fountainheads are sold with pumps in kits. Fountainheads are so inexpensive that the kit may even contain two or three.

Otherwise, you'll need to purchase your own fountainhead. Some metal fountainheads are available, but most are plastic.

When planning for your fountainhead, position it so it's well away from water lilies—they don't like to be splashed or for the water surface to be much disturbed. Also take wind into account, which will blow water from fountains that have delicate or tall sprays.

Understanding Extender Pipes

When purchasing a fountainhead, also consider the extender, the piece of (usually) plastic pipe that rises from the pump to the surface of the water, where the fountainhead snaps on. Adjust that pipe to achieve just the right height for your fountain. If needed, you can also make your own.

Crane "spitter" type fountain

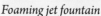

Foaming jet fountain

Daisy fountain

Many pumps and fountainheads are not sold with a length of black plastic pipe in the correct size for the fountainhead and pump extender.

And speaking of pumps, make sure that your pump is up to the task of a fountainhead. Check for a pump that has an opening specifically for fountainheads. And if you want a very tall, powerful, upward spray—more than several inches—read the packaging for both the fountainhead and pump to make sure both are up to the task

Fountain Ornaments

Fountain ornaments are a highly decorative way to also achieve the sound and sparkle of falling water. Smaller fountain ornaments are suited to small water gardens of approximately 75 gallons and under. With larger water gardens, few fountain ornaments are sufficient to provide enough aeration, so in those cases, use fountain ornaments for decoration only.

Again, read the packaging or labeling information. Look for an ornament that can move at least half the water feature's volume in an hour. Small fountain ornaments typically move 40 to 100 GPH. Larger ones typically move 100 to 400 GPH.

These types of fountains have tubing running from their bottom, concealed in the water or behind stones or edging, to a pump. The pump pushes water through the tubing and out the fountain, back into the pond.

Waterbell fountain

Understanding Container Water Gardens

Fit an entire water wonderland into a single container!

A simple container of water can have it all—a fountain, water plants, and fish. Or you can mix and match whichever elements appeal to you.

The easiest way to create a water garden is with a kit. A kit can be as complete as the container already outfitted with a fountain. Or it may be a filter and fountain with accessories that you fit into a container you purchase separately.

The container can be just about anything that will reliably hold water, though again, there are dishes and pot-like containers sold specifically for this purpose.

Smaller containers of just a gallon or so are charming, but a container garden can also be quite large. For example, whiskey barrel halves can be lined with flexible water garden liner

or large ceramic planters can be outfitted with fountains and more.

Fountains and Filters

There are a number of small fountains on the market suitable for container gardens. Look for a GPH suited to the size of your container. Be sure not to get one too powerful or you may splash water out of the container. (An adjustable output valve is worth the extra money so that you can get just the right effect.)

Many fountains have small filters built right in—especially helpful if your container garden is going to contain fish and the waste they produce. Also look for the very small container water garden filters now available.

You can allow the power cord for the fountain to simply trail over the side. Or, if you prefer, you can carefully drill a hole into the container large enough for the plug to fit through. Position the fountain and then seal with plumber's putty or epoxy to seal around the cord.

Plants

Any small plant will do well in a small container garden. Set marginal plants, such as arrowhead or dwarf papyrus planted in a small pot, at the

A plastic-lined whiskey barrel is a popular container garden. This one is outfitted with a whimsical spitter fountain that rests on the rim with the power cord trailing off the back.

bottom. Small floaters also do well. Water lilies, especially the miniature types, will thrive in larger water gardens.

Fish

Fish add life and color to a container garden. However, they do best if they have a fountain to aerate the water and provide plenty of oxygen.

Keep the number of fish limited to assure best fish health. As a rule of thumb, keep the fish small—no more than 2 or so inches—and have at least one gallon of water for each fish.

Any water garden with fish should probably be positioned in shade. Small water gardens in sun overheat quickly, and warm water can kill fish.

Container Water Garden Care

If your water garden doesn't have fish, all you'll really need to do is keep the water garden filled and occasionally tend the plants—trimming off spent or damaged foliage.

Once in a while, if the water is getting murky, simply remove most or all of the water in the container and refill.

If you want to add fish, before adding them, allow the water to set in the container for a couple of days for chemicals to dissipate. And follow all the recommended practices for water quality on pages 118–119, including using a dechlorinator as needed.

Do something similar with any water you add to the container—allow it to sit out uncovered for a day before adding to the water garden and add any necessary water conditioners. Allowing water to sit will also make sure it's the same temperature as the container, preventing fatal temperature shock for the fish.

Feed the fish sparingly but regularly as the fish food package specifies.

Solar Fountains

Check out the new solar fountains available for water gardens. They eliminate the need to hide a power cord from a fountain and also allow you to put your water garden anywhere—not just near an outdoor power outlet.

A container water garden can be as simple as a small barrel with a fountain. See page 92 for information on running an electric cord to a water feature.

Anatomy of a Disappearing Fountain

Disappearing fountains are all the latest in water features. And they're a little magical too.
Where does that water come from? And where does it go?

The name "disappearing fountain" suggests magic. But these water features are also called recirculating fountains—a little less romantic, but definitely more accurate.

Not only are disappearing fountains beautiful and pleasurable to enjoy, they're extremely safe for children.

How Disappearing Fountains Work

One of the latest trends in small water features is recirculating fountains or other elements that sit atop a tub or bucket. The container is then topped with a grate, screen, or slatted piece of strong plastic and topped with small stones or gravel. The fountain sits atop that, and a pump in the reservoir recirculates water round and round.

Basically, the decorative portion of the water fountain is placed on top of a basin set into the ground to hold a reservoir of water. The basin also holds a pump, which runs off to the side to an outdoor power outlet.

A grate or screen of some sort is positioned over the basin. On top of the grate sets the decorative urn, or millstone. It is surrounded by gravel or stones to hide the grate.

Tubing runs up from the pump into the decorative portion. Water flows up through the decoration and then splashes back down over the gravel or stones.

You can make your own disappearing fountain—sometimes called a bubbler—from scratch. Start with a millstone, a single natural stone or stack of stones (drill a hole through their center to accommodate a tube), a decorative pot, urn, or bowl, and many other objects.

Make the project even easier by starting with premade components or even a complete kit.

Creating Your Own Disappearing Fountain

The easiest way to create a disappearing fountain is by purchasing a kit, which contains all the elements needed, including a basin outfitted with the grate or covering.

The illustration here is for a disappearing fountain kit that comes complete with predrilled stones that stack on top of one another.

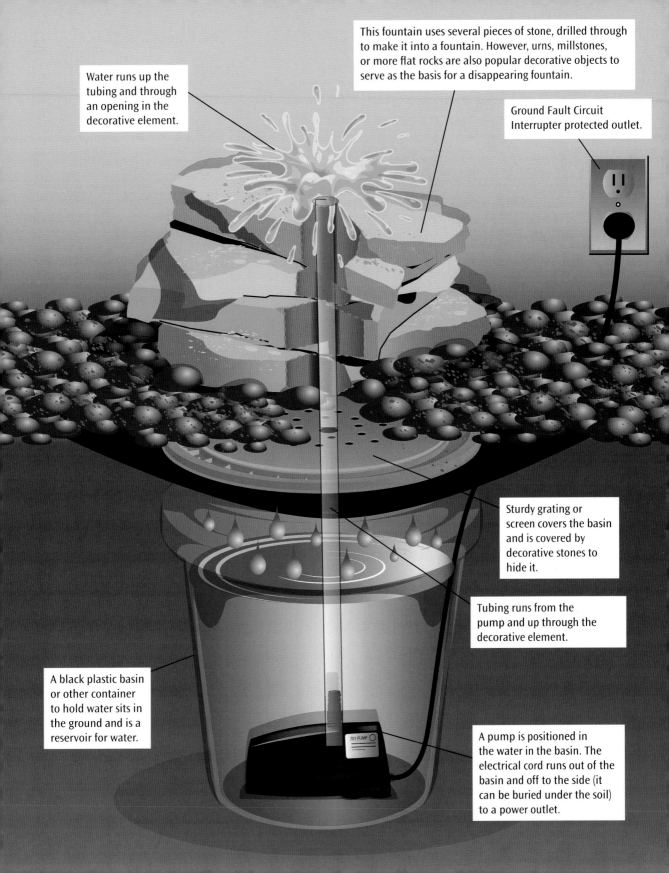

This fountain uses several pieces of stone, drilled through to make it into a fountain. However, urns, millstones, or more flat rocks are also popular decorative objects to serve as the basis for a disappearing fountain.

Water runs up the tubing and through an opening in the decorative element.

Ground Fault Circuit Interrupter protected outlet.

Sturdy grating or screen covers the basin and is covered by decorative stones to hide it.

Tubing runs from the pump and up through the decorative element.

A black plastic basin or other container to hold water sits in the ground and is a reservoir for water.

A pump is positioned in the water in the basin. The electrical cord runs out of the basin and off to the side (it can be buried under the soil) to a power outlet.

Anatomy of a Stream

A stream is basically a waterfall of some sort at the top and a pond at the bottom with a downward-sloping channel lined with flexible liner in between.

Most artificial streams contain ponds at either their head or base. These serve as reservoirs in case the pump fails and the water in the stream suddenly all runs to the bottom, which could create flooding.

A rule of thumb for designing a stream is to have twice the amount of water in the lower reservoir as the combined total of the upper pool and entire stream. Simply calculate the maximum length and the average width of the stream system and double the number for the lower reservoir.

If you don't want a visible pool, create an underground reservoir at the bottom of the stream, which will also prevent flooding in case of a pump problem. This is often called a "pondless stream."

The liner for most streams is pieced, overlapped, and sealed, so be sure to choose a liner that seams easily (see pages 52–53 for more information on liners).

Although there are no concrete rules for stream design, some basics include:

- You need some slope for a stream, but not much—just a vertical drop of 1 to 2 inches per 10 feet of length. And if you don't have that drop, you can still build up the soil to create the downward slope—just be sure to pack soil well. Under all that water and stone, soil compacts considerably.
- Always slope the streambed towards the pond.
- Create areas within the stream where the water can pool.
- If the stream narrows in one place, open it back up downstream.
- Be careful when designing a long stream without much slope. In these sorts of streams, water tends to move too slowly, causing water to well up along the sides. This can become a problem if the edges aren't high enough, so take this into account in your design.
- The most natural streams have twists and turns and work with any contours in the lands as well as existing features, such as trees, shrubs, fences, and so forth. These turns also increase the sound of rushing water—a major pleasure of a stream.
- Plan on spots for plants in the stream. They add to the natural look and are excellent filters to assure more clear water.
- Leave several inches of soil and liner above the proposed water level in the stream. It's difficult even for the pros to determine precise volume and how the water will flow. Better too deep than too shallow or your stream will overflow.
- The water depth of the stream is determined by the height of the weir in the closest downstream waterfall.
- If you want the water to move quickly, you will need to have a wider or deeper stream, or a steeper slope, or a more powerful pump.
- There are so many design variables involved in a stream that if you have a large project, it's wise to have an experienced water garden design professional review it.

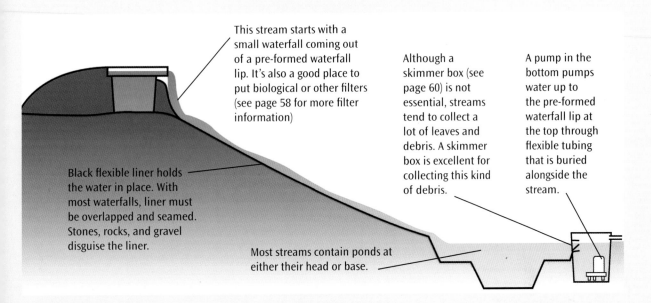

This stream starts with a small waterfall coming out of a pre-formed waterfall lip. It's also a good place to put biological or other filters (see page 58 for more filter information)

Although a skimmer box (see page 60) is not essential, streams tend to collect a lot of leaves and debris. A skimmer box is excellent for collecting this kind of debris.

A pump in the bottom pumps water up to the pre-formed waterfall lip at the top through flexible tubing that is buried alongside the stream.

Black flexible liner holds the water in place. With most waterfalls, liner must be overlapped and seamed. Stones, rocks, and gravel disguise the liner.

Most streams contain ponds at either their head or base.

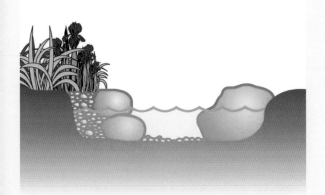

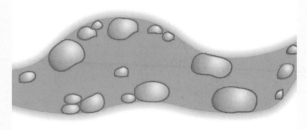

This cross-section shows how stone and gravel are used to disguise the liner. Stones not large enough to stay in place on their own are secured into place with waterfall foam. Gravel and smaller stones are then pressed into any waterfall foam that may show around the larger stones. Waterfall foam is also used underneath large stones so that the current flows easily around them and isn't trapped, which would slow the overall current of the stream.

The most natural-looking streams vary in width. Place stones of various sizes along the edges and even in the middle of the stream. With a stream, you can use a variety of these edging techniques for a more natural, interesting look. Also study the various stream photographs throughout the book. You'll see how varying widths, stones, gravel, and edges that extend gradually away from the stream are used skillfully for a "nature-must-have-put-it-there" look.

Anatomy of a Pondless Waterfall

*A pondless waterfall has all the beauty and majesty of a waterfall,
but without the danger or space needed for a pond.*

A pondless waterfall is the perfect solution for small spaces or homes with young children. It's also a great feature for a front yard because it can fit in easily to a corner or near the front door.

With a pondless waterfall, water is held in a reservoir (also called a basin) at the bottom of the falls. The basin is filled with stones, gravel, or hollow crate-like boxes that are covered with stones.

Water in the reservoir is pumped out by a pump (the cord runs off to the side to an outdoor power source). The pump propels the water through black plastic tubing up to the head of the waterfall. Gravity forces it to flow downward back into the gravel bed and the cycle begins all over again.

Keep in mind that the reservoir must have enough capacity to hold all the water should the pump fail and water suddenly rush downward into the pool.

Key design points include:

- Most basins at the bottom are not more than a couple feet deep.
- The pump often is set into a special, deeper hole just large enough to hold it to assure that it will always be surrounded with water even when water levels get low.

A pondless waterfall flows from the top of a waterfall into an underground reservoir, where water is recirculated and pumped back up to the top of the waterfall.

Usually the waterfall is created with a pre-formed waterfall with a lip, though it can run directly from tubing as well.

Flexible liner is covered with stones and gravel for the water to spill down over.

Stones and gravel create a reservoir to hold the water for the waterfall.

This pump is made specifically to be buried in the stones and gravel of a waterfall basin or hole. It has a "vault" that allows access to the pump and to check the water level in the gravel, since you'll need to add water from time to time.

More flexible liner creates a reservoir for water.

How Large Should Your Water Feature Be?

Like Goldilocks, you don't want it too big and you don't want it too small.
Here's how to get your water features sized just right for your lifestyle and needs.

Very few first-time water gardeners regret making a water feature too big. Rather, they find that they wish they had made it larger so they could have gotten even more pleasure out of it. Also, a medium-sized water feature usually takes about the same time and effort to care for as a smaller one.

Cost is a factor, and the larger the water feature, the higher the cost (see page 24 for estimating cost).

And if you're doing it yourself, you'll need to calculate how much time and skill it will take to build and maintain. Generally, smaller water features do take less skill and expertise than very large water features.

How Big Is *Big*?

Small water features, such as fountains and pools not much bigger than a luxury soaker bathtub, are great because they're easier to construct and maintain. They're also ideal for first-time water gardeners to quite literally get their feet wet and learn about the mechanics and care involved in a water garden.

Medium-sized water gardens have a surface of perhaps 10 feet by 10 feet.

Larger water gardens can take at least an hour of care a week and can be complicated to design and build, but they are more dramatic and can transform a landscape.

Whatever size water garden you're planning, it's important to know its volume. This will help you determine everything from pump power to how much of a pond product, such as an algaecide, to use. (See page 55 for more information on calculating volume.)

Sizing for Fish

If you want to have fish of any size or number, you'll need a certain minimum depth and size (see pages 136 to 140 for specifics on the needs of fish).

It's important to have enough water to support fish or the conditions will become unhealthy with too much fish waste and too much competition for oxygen.

To calculate the maximum size and number of fish you should have in your pond, figure the total surface area of the water feature.

Allow for 1 inch of fish for each 6 to 12 square inches of water. For koi, however, double that—for 1 inch of koi allow for at least 12 square inches of surface and preferably 24 square inches.

A small water feature like this can have it all—a waterfall, a pond, fish, and plants—but is far less expensive and time-consuming to build and maintain.

A pond as large as this is spectacular and truly enhances your life, whether you're hosting friends and family or enjoying a simple morning cup of coffee. But it also takes a substantial investment of money and time, not only to build but also to continue to maintain it.

Use the table below to calculate how much fish for your pond:

A 2-inch fish:	1 square foot
A 4-inch fish:	2 square feet
A 6-inch fish:	3 square feet

If you have a fountain in your pond, you can have a few more fish than if there were no fountain. A large waterfall aerates the water substantially, allowing you to have as many as double the number of fish.

Sizing for Severe Winters

If you live in an area with severe winters, and you want to overwinter fish or plants in your pond, you'll need to size your pond accordingly. Larger ponds are less likely to freeze than small ones.

If a pond contains 100 gallons, in places where temperatures don't often dip below -20°F, it probably won't freeze. In colder zones, the pond needs at least 500 gallons to assure fluid water at the bottom of the pond in severe cold.

To prevent the pond from freezing solid, it needs a deep zone.

- In areas with lows of -10°F, the deep zone should be 20 inches.
- In areas with lows of -20°F, the deep zone should be 24 inches.
- In areas with lows of -30°F, if you want to be really safe, the deep zone could be as deep as 30 inches.

How Deep Should Your Water Feature Be?

A water feature can be just an inch or two deep to a few feet deep.
Here's how to determine the best depth for your water feature.

The style of your water garden and how you plan to use it is what will dictate depth. Obviously, a feature like a flat-bottomed reflecting pool needs only an inch or two of water. But if you want plants and fish, or if you live in a cold climate and want to make sure your pond doesn't freeze, you'll need to do some more detailed design.

Designing for Plants

Many favorite water garden plants are "marginals," that is, they do best with their roots submerged in the water and their foliage above the water. (See page 128 for more information on marginals.) In nature, these plants grow in bogs and shallows. In most water gardens, grow them in pots set onto "shelves" built into the water feature.

The shelf can be as shallow as just a couple of inches or as deep as 18 inches, depending on the size of pots you plan to use for your marginal plants. Design shelves so they are about an inch or so deeper than the pots.

If you have enough space in the deep zone—usually 2 feet—you can also overwinter marginal plants in this unfrozen water.

Some water gardeners, instead of using pots, like to plant in bog gardens or in planting pockets created with stone and moist soil. This is ideal for plants that are cold-hardy to your area (meaning they don't need to be overwintered in a deep zone or indoors).

Water Lilies

Water lilies come in a variety of heights, with miniatures growing just a foot or so high and taller types growing as tall as 3 feet.

When starting water lilies outdoors in the spring, some growers recommend first setting them on a marginal shelf about 6 inches deep and then moving them, as they grow, to a depth of 12 to 18 inches.

Designing for Fish

If you live in a climate where temperatures regularly plunge below freezing for extended periods of time, you'll want to create a deeper zone where the water won't freeze and fish can overwinter.

"Deep zones" for fish should be at least 18 inches deep, but you can go as deep as 30 inches if you live in a very cold (USDA Zone 5 and below) region and want to be sure.

Be sure to make the deep zone large enough to accommodate fish in the number and size you want.

Shallow plant shelf for marginal plants, 1 to 8 inches tall

Mid-zone for water lilies and larger marginal plants, about 8 to 12 inches tall

Deep zone for fish and extremely large or tall plants, up to 2 feet tall

Consult a Pro

Designing a stream is one of the trickier bits of water garden design. It's important to have just the right overall volume, reservoir for water in case of pump failure, slope, and pump power. Also, streams that aren't designed well tend to overflow on the sides, creating significant water loss. Even the pros can struggle a bit with stream design.

A badly designed stream can have too little flow and look stagnant. Or it doesn't hold water well and looks like a rather sad semi-dry streambed with lots of liner showing.

Therefore, it's a really good idea to consult with a pro on your design. Take it to a water garden supply store and consult with staff there. They'll likely give you a quick assessment of the design for no fee. Even if there is a more extensive review needed, they may do it for no charge in the hopes that you'll buy supplies from them either now or in the future. Or seek out a water garden designer. Ask them if they'll review the design and troubleshoot for a small flat fee. Considering a stream costs several hundred to a few thousand dollars and many days to build, this investment in a sound design is well worth it.

Working with Stone

Stone adds character and timelessness to your water feature.
Learn how to choose it and use it effectively.

Choosing Stone

- As much as possible, use local stone. It looks more natural in your landscape—because it is. Lava rocks in the Midwest can look silly.
- Choose stone of the same type and color as much as possible to achieve a unified look. If you're using granite boulders, for example, avoid mixing them with cut limestone pavers.
- Stone collected from local land (if you own it or have permission) is fine for many water features.
- When purchasing stone, it's worth your time to handpick larger stones yourself, rather than relying on the supplier to do it. Only you know exactly the look you're going for.
- Don't be timid about using large stones. They can truly anchor your water garden and make it look substantial.
- When buying stone, also buy shims—tiny flat pieces used to level larger stones.

Working with Stone

- Wear workboots, preferably steel-toed. Also use heavy gloves—padded gloves are ideal.
- If you'll be kneeling a lot, rubber knee pads can save wear and tear on clothes, skin, and strained knees.
- If you have a choice between pushing and pulling on a rock, push. It's less strain on your back.

Tools and Techniques

- If you're having a load of stone delivered on your driveway, lay down some old plywood or even just a couple layers of heavy cardboard in the form of cut-down boxes to protect it.
- Invest in or rent a dolly cart for moving stones back and forth. It's a major labor saver and ideal for flagstone and other flat stone.
- Some large stones can be moved by putting them on a folded sturdy tarp and dragging them (with a friend's help, if needed) across paving or grass.
- A long prybar is the ideal tool for moving very large boulders.
- If some stones are too large for you to place easily, talk to the place that sold you the stone. They may position them for you for a reasonable fee. Then you can place the other smaller stones yourself.
- As you work, place the largest stones first.
- Embed any stone larger than a softball as much as you can in soil, smaller stones, and/or gravel. This mimics nature, where few boulders are just lying on top of the soil. For a natural look, try to bury larger stones and boulders by as little as one third and as much as one half.

With the right technique and tools, moving this many large stones and boulders may be easier than you think.

Using Limestone

Be cautious when using limestone. It may affect the pH of your garden. If it's hard, dense, or weathered, it's probably fine. Softer limestone, however, can leach pH-altering minerals into the water. If in doubt, pour a little vinegar on the stone. If it foams and bubbles profusely, don't use it. If the reaction is only slight, it's fine to use.

Understanding Edging

Edging for any water garden is critical. It needs to help hold the liner in place but also disguise it for a finished, professional look.

Edging is essential to a water feature's good looks—helping it blend into its surrounding and hiding the less-attractive liners but it also does so much more: Edging holds the liner in place. And when well installed, it helps protect the liner from destructive UV rays from the sun. It can help prevent soil and debris from washing into the water garden.

Types of Edging

When deciding on an edging material, take into account other materials already in your hardscape. If there's a lot of brick, consider that material. If there's already naturalistic flagstone, try some more of that.

Mix and match stones carefully. Limestone and granite together can look jarring, unless very carefully done. Also even the same type of stone, such as limestone, can have very different coloring. Buy all your stone in one group, if you can.

Materials for edging include:
- Flagstones
- Cut stone
- Rounded boulders of all sizes
- Brick
- Pavers
- A combination of boulders and smaller stones and gravel

One of the simplest ways to edge a pond is with a ring of large stones. Mix in some pebbles and smaller stones for a more natural look.

This type of edging creates an even more natural look since it hides more of the liner farther below the water surface.

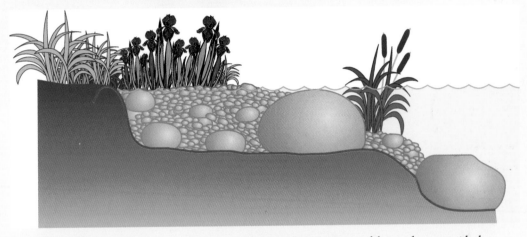

To create a wetlands or bog area, install this type of edging along a portion of the pond to create ideal conditions for marginal plants.

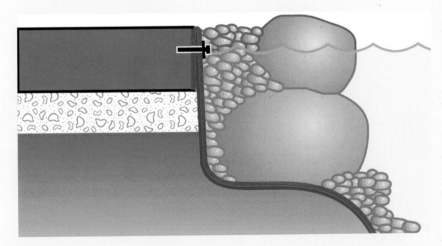

When putting a water feature up against a concrete patio, use a combination of aluminum strips and bolts.

Plumbing Basics

Plumbing for water gardens can be very simple or very involved. If you're a first-time water garden builder, you'll want to keep it simple. Here are the key components you're likely to use.

Flexible PVC Tubing

The tubing of choice for most pond building today, this black flexible tubing can run water up along a waterfall, handles sharp turns, is tough, and withstands weather extremes. Choose the type with a smooth interior so water flow isn't slowed.

Rigid PVC is still used in some water garden projects. But it comes in only 10- and 20-foot increments, needs special elbow joints to navigate turns, and isn't quite as resistant to freezing as flexible PVC. Use sealant to attach joints, valves, and elbows. Use Schedule 40 rigid PVC for water features.

Check or One-Way Valve

This is used to prevent back flush from a filter, preserving valuable bacterial growth that has built up in the filter.

Coupling

Fits two pieces of pipe together. Shown here is a coupler for rigid PVC, which requires the use of solvent cement. The same coupling can be used for flexible PVC, but the solvent cement needs to work with flexible PVC.

Ball Valve

This reduces water flow through the pipe.

Manifold

This splits flow from one pipe into two. Its design creates far less head loss than a standard T fitting.

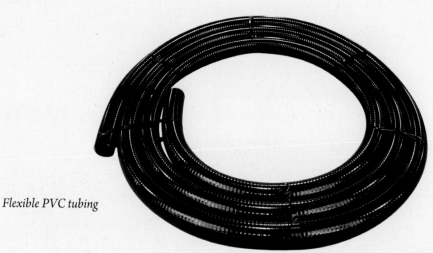

Flexible PVC tubing

Check valve

Ball valve

Coupling

Manifold

Avoid Polyethylene (PE) Pipe

Avoid using large-diameter polyethylene pipe—a type of black plastic tubing. There are much better options these days for water gardens. The barbed fittings can be difficult to insert properly and the metal clamps needed are inconvenient.

Understanding Electrical Elements

Let there be light—and pumps and waterfalls and filters and more!
Electricity is what powers all of these for a healthy, low-maintenance water feature.

Electricity is needed to power pumps, waterfalls, pond heaters, filters, and in some cases runs lighting. It's also useful to have on hand in using power equipment around your water feature.

Most water features run on a standard 120-volt household current. A very large feature might need a 220-volt dedicated circuit, the type used for major household appliances such as clothes dryers or air conditioners.

GFCI outlets

Ground-Fault Circuit Interrupter (GFCI) outlets are a critical safety feature for any outdoor electrical use. You'll see them in bathrooms and kitchens where water is used, and they have a little reset (usually red) button in the center.

The GFCI senses any electrical contact with water as well as any overload, and instantly stops the current, preventing bad shocks and even electrocution.

Any power outlet installed outdoors these days must be GFCI. If you live in an older home, you may come across some ungrounded outlets, but do not use them for a water feature.

If you have a GFCI outlet within 6 to 10 or so feet (the length of most water feature electrical cords) of where you want your water garden, you're set.

Otherwise, you'll need to have one installed. (If you use an extension cord, make sure that it is rated for external use.) GFCI boxes can be mounted on fence posts or other permanent

objects, or installed freestanding just a few inches above the ground, hidden behind plants.

Although an experienced amateur can often install this, local electrical codes may require a licensed professional. Expect to spend about $200 to $400, depending on the rates of the electrician and the distance from the electrical source.

Also consider how much additional load you'll be putting on your circuit box. A 15-amp circuit can handle a continuous load of 1440 watts. A 20-amp circuit can handle 1920.

If you have any doubts, check with an electrician to be sure.

Ground-Fault Circuit Interrupter (GFCI) outlets are a safe, reliable way to provide power to your water feature.

Working with Foam

It used to be that rocks and other heavy objects in water gardens were anchored with mortar. Today, it's faster, easier, more efficient, and more attractive to use waterfall foam.

Waterfall foam comes in a pressurized can and, like insulation foam, expands when released. It anchors stones in place, and fills voids between the rocks and liner, diverting water around and over stones. It's far easier to use than mortar and won't crack in freezing temperatures. And while the goal is for it to be completely covered with stonework, its black color blends in, looking like stone or shadow.

When dry, if necessary, it can be peeled or cut or trimmed away—much like soft Styrofoam—but this is a last resort.

There's a skill to using waterfall foam. Some tips for best results:

- Because of its quickly expanding nature, waterfall foam can be a little hard to control until you get the hang of it. If you've never used it before, experiment with it a bit first before working on your actual project.

- Wear disposable gloves. It sticks to skin and can be nearly impossible to get out from underneath nails. (Use a pumice stone to remove any that gets on your skin.)

- For small projects, working directly from a one-time use can is fine. However, for larger projects, invest in a foam gun with a long pin-point barrel. It allows you to work more precisely between stones and allows instant shut-off of the foam. (Also invest in foam gun cleaner!)

- Foam adheres better to damp surfaces than dry. Moisten (but don't soak) stones and liner before hand for ideal contact.

- With larger stones and boulders, apply a thin layer of black foam underneath and on the sides of each stone. Use only a thin coat because the foam will expand.

Foam gun

Understanding Lighting

*Lighting adds drama and hours of additional enjoyment to your water feature—
and it's easy to do it yourself!*

*Even small water features can benefit from lighting.
Three low-voltage spotlights shine up to make the
water glow as it spills out of this urn.*

Almost every water garden needs some lighting or another. After all, lights and water are a magical combination that plays off each other beautifully. Also, unlike the regular garden, a water feature sometimes is best enjoyed at night *because* of the lights. And it's also cooler and quieter at night, making for a more relaxing experience.

Some water garden lighting operates off a standard 120-volt household current. This type of lighting usually requires considerable electrical experience or even a licensed electrician to install (check local code, which may require it).

However, the popularity of low-voltage lighting has exploded in the past few years and for good reason—it's easy to install yourself.

When thinking about adding lighting to your water feature, be aware of the different types:

Floating

Floating lights drift atop the water, like little floating luminarias. They are anchored at the bottom of the pool or pond with anchors supplied with the lights. Some are simple and elegant, such as frosted white globes, and others are novelties, such as illuminated lily pads.

Submerged

Submerged lights can be used in several ways. Available both as floodlights or spotlights, they are—as the name suggests—installed under the water. Often a spotlight is beamed up out of the water to highlight a statue or dramatic plant.

This water feature has a couple of submerged lights tucked under edging to create a soft glow. But since water reflects light so beautifully, the surface also is reflecting the lighting on the house.

Submerged lights can also be put under fountains or waterfalls and shone upward to make the moving water appear to glow.

Floodlight

Floodlights can be used in water or outside the water feature. On dry land, they're excellent for lighting a large area, such as a seating area. Or they can be used as uplights underneath a large feature, such as a tree, with the extra light illuminating the whole area. In the water, they can be used to illuminate an entire pool. Just be sure to direct the beam away from where people will be observing the pool, or it might create glare.

Spotlight

Spotlights also can be used in or out of the water. Use them to shine upward to highlight a statue or a tree, but unlike a floodlight, there will be less scattered light to illuminate the whole area.

Fountain Spray Lights

Among the showiest of water feature lighting, pond jets (also called fountain spray lights) dramatically illuminate a fountain. Choose from

A single submerged light illuminates this whole pool.

white or other colors. These floating lights are sold in sets of three or more or in a kit, often with a submersible pump and a timer, which work in tandem with the lights themselves.

Landscape Lights

Regular lighting in the garden can also be used around the water feature. Footlights are wonderful surrounding a pond or stream edge. They're also useful to provide safety and beauty along porches, paths, and decks near water features.

Low-Voltage Lighting

Unlike regular electrical features, low-voltage systems are safe and easy for even beginners to install (see pages 114–115).

Tiered lights, also called pagoda lights, are widely available and the most popular type of low-voltage light. They provide downlight along paths and driveways and are striking when surrounding a pool or pond.

Low-voltage lights also are available as spotlights and floodlights. They're also available as submerged lighting and floating lighting.

Light-emiting diode (LED) bulbs are highly efficient and last a decade or more. They cost more, but pay for themselves in energy efficiency.

One of the simplest, most dramatic ways to light a water feature is with a submerged light behind the waterfall to illuminate the water as it falls. It's like watching liquid light cascade.

∽ 4 ∽

Building Your Water Feature

*Y*OUR RESEARCH IS DONE; YOUR MATERIALS AND SUPPLIES ARE secured. Time to quite literally dig in and start installing your water feature!

A small project can take a matter of hours; a somewhat larger project might take a weekend. If you've been really ambitious, you may be embarking on a project that even with help might take several days—or even weeks.

In this chapter, you'll find detailed information about how to actually assemble your water garden, from the first hit of the spade on the soil to positioning the last stone along the edge before filling. Enjoy!

How to Dig the Hole & Achieve Level

This job can be a snap or quite challenging, depending on the size and condition of the soil. When installing a water garden, the adage could be "Check level twice, dig once."

Follow these tips to dig smart, saving your back and your time.

- At least a couple of weeks before you dig, contact your city or other local government to have all pipes and lines flagged or marked. (There's usually no charge.) This prevents hitting them when you're digging. In the U.S., you can simply call 811 in any state and you will be directed to the appropriate local authority to make an appointment.

- A few days before you plan to excavate, dig an "exploratory" hole or two a couple feet wide and as deep as your water garden. This will let you determine if there are many rocks, clay, hardpan, or roots and allow you to plan accordingly.

- If the area has lots of roots, keep a mattock, a long-handled lopper, and a small saw on hand to work through the roots.

- In areas with hardpan or clay, soak the area thoroughly the day before with water to soften the clay. If the soil is very dry, you may need to water twice in two days.

- In clay soils, use a fiberglass-handled round-point shovel—it won't break as easily. In severe clay hardpan, try a pick axe.

- Hoist large rocks out with a long-handled pry bar and remove them with the help of a friend. If you hit one that's immovable, consider designing around it (easy to do with flexible liner).

- For larger projects, consider renting a backhoe or ditch digger. Rentals are usually reasonably priced.

Tools and Supplies

Round-point shovel

Flat-edged shovel

Wheelbarrow

Tarp (optional)

Trowel

Pick-axe (for hardpan or dry clay soils)

Rented jackhammer (for rocky or severe hardpan soils)

Heavy work gloves

Heavy work boots

1

Mark the Outline

Use spray paint or a garden hose or stakes and twine to mark the outline. Keep spray paint on hand since you'll be using it for any additional layers to be added to the pool.

2

Start Excavating

If you are creating shelves and different depths, dig out the first layer of soil of the water garden, that is, the overall shape down to the first ledge. Check the level as you work.

Pile soil on a driveway, patio, or on a tarp on the lawn.

Repeat the marking process for the second and any third level of the water garden, mark where the shelves or ledges should be. As needed, use a flat-edged shovel or hand trowel to shape the ledge. They are more precise than a round-point shovel. Check the level again.

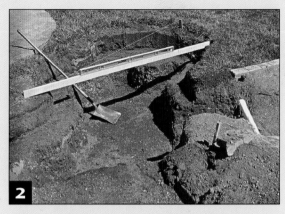

2

Repeat the process for any third, deeper level. As you work, remember to allow space for 1 to 2 inches of sand you may be using under a rigid liner.

Protecting the Electric Cord

As long as you've got the shovel out, it's a good time to dig a trench for an electric cord. There are many ways to provide electrical power to operate the fountain pump. The best way is to add a new outdoor circuit, but this requires an electrician if you are not experienced with home wiring. The easier route is to feed your fountain pump with an exterior-rated extension cord that's plugged into an existing outdoor receptacle. Because having an extension cord lying in your lawn is both a tripping hazard and an electrical hazard (lawn mowers and wiring do not get along), you can bury the cord in a shallow trench. To protect it from digging instruments, either backfill with rocks so you know the exact location of the cord, or bury it encased in heavy conduit.

Avoid using this tactic if the pond is located more than 50 feet from the power source.

Tips for a Perfect Level

Getting your water garden excavated with perfect level is critical. Water always seeks to be level, so if you dig one end a little deeper or higher than the other, it will be painfully apparent once you fill the feature with water. This is especially true with a rigid liner, formal pond, or highly regular edging (such as brick). With flexible liner, if things are a little off, you can cover up mistakes to some minor degree with artfully placed stone and gravel. But with a rigid liner, that's not usually possible.

Follow these tips to achieve perfect level every time:

- Use the right level for the job. That 8-inch-long level you use around the house for small projects just won't cut it. The longer the level, the more precise it is over a distance. For a water garden project, use a 48-inch-long level.

  Then set the level on a perfectly straight piece of lumber, stretched across the pool, pond, or streambed.

- For large projects, you can stretch string straight across, taut, and use a line level or hold the level along the string. But this technique has limited precision. For a more accurate (and easier) reading of level, invest in a laser level.

- Take your time. Getting level is important. You may need to backfill or redo—but it will be time well spent. If you're installing a rigid liner, be prepared to remove it as many times as needed to get it perfectly straight.

- Check level throughout the project. Be meticulous and check frequently while digging and each time you seat items such as a skimmer or pre-formed waterfall unit.

- As you work, tamp down sand and soil evenly. The weight of the water and any stones can settle soil by as much as an inch or two. Tamp down firmly and evenly to make sure your water feature isn't level when you install it but then settles unevenly and is no longer level.

Disposing of Leftover Soil

Soil from excavation can be used to level the area around the water feature or to build a grade for a stream or waterfall. Otherwise, good-quality topsoil can be spread elsewhere in the landscape, especially into raised beds and berms.

Subsoil (the lesser-quality soil underneath the topsoil that is usually laden with clay) or other problem soils aren't suitable for growing things, so you'll need to dispose of it. As you dig, pile the soil on the driveway or other paved area or on a tarp spread out on the grass (remove the tarp in a day or two or you'll kill the grass).

Waste disposal services sometimes will provide a special oversized dumpster-like box into which you can load the excess dirt that they'll haul away. Or check want ads or online for "fill dirt"—someone may take it from you for no charge to use in construction projects. Otherwise, contact an excavation, contractor, or landscaping company about hauling it away for a fee.

How to Install a Flexible Liner

Flexible liner has become extremely popular because it's fast and easy to install. Find out for yourself!

Once you've dug the hole, now comes the easy part: installing the flexible liner. For any water feature more than a few yards across, it's good to have a helper or even two or three to help with this process. Liner is surprisingly heavy—a 10 by 20 piece weighs about 80 pounds! And, as with making a big bed, it's useful to have someone on the other side, helping to arrange things so you don't have to walk several feet for every tweak and tug.

Flexible liner is more pliable in warm conditions, so try to time your project for a sunny day that is at least 65° F. Spread out the liner, as much as space permits, and allow it to warm in the sun for an hour or two.

Tools and Supplies

- Heavy-duty scissors
- Garden hose attached to spigot
- Flexible liner
- Underlayment
- Double-sided EDPM joint tape
- Aquarium-grade silicone sealant
- Washed gravel, boulders, and edging materials

Position the Underlayment

Use an underlayment made specifically for water gardens to prevent punctures and tears in the liner itself. Position the underlayment as precisely as you can into the water garden.

Position the Liner

Spread the liner over the underlayment, smoothing any wrinkles. If seams are necessary, follow the seaming instructions recommended for that type of liner. Different liners require different techniques, but most suggest overlapping the pieces by 18 inches and sealing with a compatible double-sided EPDM joint tape.

Weight the liner with stones to hold it in place as you work to position it. Where practical, add an inch or two of water to the bottom to help it settle more firmly into the hole.

3

Add Accessories

Position any accessories that affect the liner, such as skimmer boxes or premade waterfall forms. Connect the liner to these following instructions from the manufacturer of each accessory. Most recommend using an aquarium-grade silicone sealant on all joints and fastening parts with corrosion-resistant fasteners (such as stainless steel) to avoid leaks.

Trim the liner, leaving a 2-foot margin along the edges.

4

Position Gravel, Stones, and Edging

As much as is practical, cover the liner with a layer of washed stones and gravel to protect it from punctures and the destructive UV rays of the sun. Add more water if practical.

Add other stones and edging before making any final trims to the liner.

4

Troubleshooting Liner Installation

So what happens if you dig the hole, position the liner, and . . . it's too small? Frustrating as this is, it's best to immediately contact the business that sold you the liner. Chances are, they'll accept the return and exchange it for a larger liner.

If it's a custom-made liner, returns will be more problematic. If the company won't allow a credit for the purchase of the right-sized liner, consider selling it on eBay. Liners can cost hundred of dollars and there are always Internet-savvy shoppers looking for a bargain.

What you definitely *shouldn't* do is to try to seam together pieces of trim to make the liner fit. Many seams in unprotected areas are highly likely to leak in a matter of a few years—if not months.

How to Install a Rigid Liner Pond

*A rigid liner takes much of the guesswork out of pond design—it's already determined for you.
Just set into it the ground and fill with water!*

A rigid liner is appealing to many just getting started in water gardening. It's simple to wrap your brain around design and installation, and therefore most liners are small, targeted at beginning water gardens.

However, rigid liners are not without their drawbacks. Getting them (and keeping them) level over the years can be challenging. Also, if you want a natural look, the rigid edge is tricky to conceal.

But for many first-time water gardeners, rigid liners are the perfect way to truly dip their toes into the world of water gardening.

Tools and Supplies

Spades

Rope

Rigid liner

Sand

Level

Long, straight piece of lumber

Compactable gravel (optional)

Tamping tool (optional)

Stone for edging, as desired

Outline the Pond

Using the level or another straight-edged tool, mark the edge of the liner on the ground with a rope.

Dig the Pond

Cut away any existing sod and reuse as desired. Measure the depth of the liner at the center and excavate the base to that depth. Dig the hole 2″ to 3″ deeper than the liner and past the edges of the outline by a couple of inches. Match the contours of the liner as closely as possible so the marginal shelves will be supported by soil and sand.

Position the Liner

Remove any rocks or roots and cover the bottom with 1 to 2 inches of sand. Set the liner in place to see how well it fits and adjust the sand on the underside until the liner rim is slightly above the ground. Test, level, and adjust. Be sure to use ample sand so no settling occurs. Also, be sure the level is exact. Water *always* is level, so if the liner is positioned even slightly off, it will be obvious.

If the pond is small, you may want to double-check the level by filling partly or fully with water. Empty the pond by at least half by bailing with a bucket as much as you can and proceed. (Some water will help anchor the pond.)

3

4

Tamp in the Soil and Sand

Fill in around the sides with a mixture of soil and sand. Use a trowel and hands to pack it in firmly, dampening with water as you go to further settle the sand.

If you are adding edging and compactable gravel, leave room for those elements.

5

Adding Edging Stones

Stones, concrete pavers, or other edging may be added for a decorative touch or to disguise the lip of the liner.

This edging is being placed on top of a layer of compactable gravel to hold them more

steadily than sand and soil would. Layer the gravel 1 to 2 inches deep, and then tamp down firmly. Using a tamping tool is ideal.

Edging can be just one course (layer) or two, overlapping as desired to further disguise the lip. However, the stone must not press down heavily on the lip or it can damage it.

Be sure to arrange the cord of any pumps, filters, or fountains among the edging so that you can remove the cord easily for maintenance.

Good Idea!

For a more natural look, pour a layer of pea gravel or small stones in the bottom of the liner.

Installing Edging

Edging is one of your water feature's most prominent elements, so be sure to do it right.

There are many different types of edging, but coping stones around the rim are among the most popular and enduring.

Tools and Supplies

- Various stones and rock
- Concrete mortar and/or waterfall foam
- Trowel
- Level
- Rubber mallet
- Sponge
- Garden hose attached to spigot
- Submersible utility pump or clean-out pump

Loosely Position Stones Along Edges

Position smaller stones in the deeper parts with larger stones holding them in place. Also place edging stones on top so they'll be positioned 1 to 2 inches above the water and hanging 2 to 3 inches over the edge, sloping away from the edge, so they don't fall into the pond and so they divert runoff away from the pond.

Securing Stones in Place

Depending on the design of your water garden, you can use mortar or waterfall foam (see page 83 for tips on working with foam). If using mortar, working in small sections, remove each stone to create a bed of mortar. Moisten the stone and then loosely seat it in the mortar bed.

Again position the edging stones to hang 2 to 3 inches over the edge. Make sure the stones are level with each other and slope away from the pool. Tap the edging stones firmly into the mortar, using a rubber mallet.

Set Stones Around the Fixtures

If you are using skimmer boxes, large filters, and other fixtures, fit stones loosely around them to help them blend in in a pleasing manner. Replace any utility covers and make sure they fit over the stones. Do not put any stones permanently over pipe fittings or electrical connections.

While you could use mortar for this part of the project, waterfall foam is especially effective in this application. Otherwise, working in a small section at a time, mix mortar and create a bed for the stones. Position the stones and tap them into place, using a rubber mallet.

4

Clean the Stones

Use water and a damp sponge to remove any mortar spills or excess. If using foam, allow it to dry 5 minutes, then push it back in place or cut away excess. Or press stones or gravel into any foam that oozes out from behind larger rocks.

With mortar, allow it to set for 24 hours. Then fill the pond or stream, using a submersible utility pump or clean-out pump to extract water contaminated by mortar or debris. (This is far less of a problem with waterfall foam.)

5

Fill the Feature

Once the dirty water is adequately removed, fill the water feature with clean water. You will probably need to adjust the pump to achieve just the right flow. Also fine-tune stone placement. Add or remove loose stones, including adding some in the middle of the stream to mimic water features in nature. Check the edges of the stream liner to make sure the water isn't overflowing in any place. If it is, lift the edge and backfill with soil as much as is practical.

Then plant the feature. Remember that unless you've created a bog-type edge in places, the plants next to a stream won't necessarily receive more moisture than other plants in your garden. But do choose those that look at home on the side of the stream.

Good choices include perennials such as iris, ornamental grasses, ferns, hydrangeas, astilbe, columbine, daffodils, heuchera, creeping and woodland phlox, hostas, lamium, azaleas, and rhododendrons.

How to Build a Waterfall

Start with a ready-made waterfall unit and then simply add stones.

Calculating the type of pump and head and lift needed for a waterfall is science. But laying the stone for a waterfall is art.

A pre-formed waterfall unit can take out a lot of the guesswork. But when it comes to regulating water flow—especially upstream and adjusting stones and rocks so that the water splashes over them just right—it's a matter of working with the shape and size of the rocks for the effect that is most pleasing to you.

Anatomy of a Waterfall

A pre-made waterfall unit holds a reservoir of water and creates a solid base on which to position stones.

The spill stone is the stone that the water flows over, supported underneath by the foundation stone.

A foundation stone supports the spill stone, usually along the front of the waterfall unit.

Gate stones are located on either side of the waterfall and stream to help channel water over the spill stone and downward.

Tips For Building the Perfect Waterfall

Consider the terrain. If your backyard is flat, a waterfall that pops up out of nowhere will not look natural. If necessary, modify the terrain somewhat by building a berm a few feet high. For the most natural look with a waterfall, create several smaller drops of 4 to 9 inches or one drop of no more than 18 inches.

Proportion stones with the drop of the waterfall in mind. The main rocks along the side of the waterfall boulders should be a few to several inches larger than the drop of the waterfall. For example, for a drop of 12 inches, you should use rocks that are 16 inches across.

Use gate stones. Use some of the largest stones in the project to frame the waterfall. These stones channel the water to the waterfall, over the waterfall, and then can keep it in check as it flows farther down.

Go fewer and bigger. Fewer rocks are better when building a waterfall. Three large stones are better than 12 small stones stacked up. In nature, you usually find one very large stone, surrounded by few smaller ones, with the water running between them.

Design twists and turns. Create these in the waterfall and stream so that there are new views and facets with every turn. They also improve sound.

Add plants. The more plant material you use to line the falls and stream, the better. They soften raw, hard edges and make the waterfall look like it has always been there.

Use larger gate stones on the either side of a waterfall with foundation stones underneath the lip. The foundation stone is topped with the spill stone, over which water flows and falls.

Tools and Supplies

- Pre-formed waterfall unit
- Shovel
- Level
- Flexible liner
- Double-sided EPDM joint tape
- Mortar and/or waterfall foam
- Assorted stones and rocks

1

Start with a Pre-formed Waterfall Unit

You can build a waterfall without one, but these make the job much easier by giving you a solid base structure and built-in reservoir. Position it at the top of the waterfall or stream. Bonus: You can put filters inside of the reservoir to make the unit do double duty.

2

Lay the Liner

Position the flexible liner along the stream, attaching it to the waterfall unit as directed by the unit manufacturer. Aquarium-grade silicone is usually recommended as a sealant. Seal pieces as needed, following the liner manufacturer's instructions, but usually with EPDM tape and 18-inch overlap. Position any seams under a waterfall so that the top piece overlaps the bottom piece.

3

Start Positioning the Stones

Put the foundation stones in place first, using mortar or expandable waterfall foam. (Have smaller stones nearby to set into any waterfall foam that shows.) Top with the spill stone and then position with various gate stones.

4

Fill In With Smaller Stones

Use cobblestones and other small stones strategically to disguise the foam holding the larger stones in place.

5

Add Gravel and More Stones

Cover the liner with washed gravel and cobblestones.

Building a Stream

Building a stream certainly is ambitious in terms of square footage, but because it's shallow, the digging requirement is somewhat easier than others. The challenging part is creating a stream that's the right depth and width to get just the effect of moving water you want.

As you build your stream, work with your landscape. If you've designed it well, it will look as though it's always been there.

But design can go only so far. In designing a stream, as you work, you'll need to frequently check level and depth to execute your plans. Also, digging a stream can be a very organic process. You will find yourself digging away and piling back soil to make it wide or narrow just right or to get a perfectly pleasing twist in its course.

When it comes to stone placement, you'll also have to be very intuitive. Be prepared to arrange and rearrange stones so they look just right. The end result will be a stream that functions beautifully, with just the right amount of water you want flowing at just the right speed, for a restful and attractive backyard showpiece.

1

Dig the Stream Bed

After determining the best site for your stream, preferably one that has at least a slight slope, mark out the course of your stream.

Besides the channel of the stream, you'll also need to dig out a place for a pre-formed waterfall unit at the stream's head, and any pool or pond at the stream's head.

Also dig a pond or reservoir at the foot of the stream large enough to capture all or most of the water that the stream will hold. This is crucial because if the pump fails for any reason, all the water of the feature will rush downhill and flood an undersized pond.

As you work with soil, also take into account any waterfalls you have planned for the stream. As much as possible, work with the grade and shape of the land to incorporate these falls. (See page 68 for more stream design tips. See page 107 for waterfall design tips.)

Note that the stream shown here isn't just a simple channel with sides that cut straight down. Instead, there are more shallow portions around the edges, creating the perfect platform on which to nestle boulders, gravel, and small stones. And even those shallow portions aren't highly regular. They are wider and narrower in some parts as well as deeper or more shallow, gradually blending into the lawn, in others.

As you dig, allow for about 2 inches of soil settling over time. Loose soil compacts considerably under the weight of the water and boulders.

2

Line the Stream Bed

Spread the underlayment over the streambed. Then top with flexible liner. With a stream, you will likely have to piece sections of flexible liner together. The best place to do this is where a

waterfall is located so the top piece can overlap the bottom piece. (See page 94 for how to work with and seam flexible liner.)

Hold the liner in place by starting to place the largest boulders and rocks. These larger rocks will take center stage with all the other rocks balancing and supporting the basic composition they create.

3

Finishing Stonework, Filling, and Planting

After placing the major large stones in and along your stream, add the smaller boulders and gravel. Go for a random look, the way you would find in nature. Use a good mix of different sizes of stone and gravel to create a natural look.

Wherever elevation changes significantly, place some larger stones or a series of stones. This replicates the look of erosion that happens in nature wherever water is moving downward.

In a stream, use waterfall foam to secure stones only where the water drops. Otherwise, most are fine being held in place by simple gravity.

It's smart to add plants to your stream. They are excellent filters for better water quality and help the stream fit into its surroundings.

Plants can be positioned right next to the stream, on the soil side of the liner. These help the feature visually blend naturally into the landscape, but they do not help filter the water. Also, some gardeners mistakenly think that because a plant is next to a water feature, it will get additional water, but that's not necessarily true unless there is regularly overflow—not a good thing!

Consider creating a bog edge or bog pocket planting alongside the stream. Position several of these along the stream for a natural look. They can be small or extensive. They can be shaped so they are long, narrow, and follow along a length of the stream or are more rounded and extending out away from the stream. Choose "marginal" plants for your bog garden—plants that are naturally suited to wet, marshy conditions. See page 128 for more information on marginal plants.

Good Idea!

Be prepared to adjust and redo as needed. The larger the project, the more difficult it is to predict exactly how water will flow, given all the variables in each stream. A pro tells a story about building a stream more than 300 feet long, but with very little grade change. He allowed for more than 8 inches of liner above the predicted water level, but the stream still backed up and overflowed its banks. He had to rework a 50-foot section of the upper stream to keep the water in place.

3

How to Install Low-Voltage Lighting

While regular household currents are dangerous to work with, low-voltage lighting is easy, safe, and takes just an hour or so to install.

A low-voltage system uses a safe 12-volt system instead of the more powerful, hazardous 120-volt standard household system. It's ideal for landscape and water garden lighting, and these days there is a wide variety of lights to choose from: tiered, spotlights, underwater lights, floodlights, and more.

Kits are the easiest way to go. For as little as $100, you can buy a kit complete with the transformer (the box that converts currents), an ample amount of wire, connectors, and plenty of lights. It may even contain a timer so your lights go off and on exactly when you want them to.

Transformers are the heart of the system. Mount these boxes on a wall or post next to a GFCI outlet—which is on the regular 120-volt household current. Then simply plug the transformer into the outlet. The transformer lowers the voltage to just 12 volts.

Transformers in kits are usually designed to handle just the lights or equipment included in the kit. Any additions will overload the kit transformer.

So you may want to buy the transformer separately so it can accommodate the lights and accessories you want. First calculate equipment and lights you want to use and total the wattage. Buy a transformer that can handle an extra 50 percent of the total to accommodate any adds after the project is done.

1

Install the transformer to a GFCI outlet, following the instructions that come with it. Then dig a trench and lay the cable for the lighting (also included in most kits, or you can purchase separately) between the transformer and the edge of the water feature.

2

Connect the cable at the transformer.

3

Adjust and position the lights (inset). Then adjust and set the automatic timer.

Tools and Supplies

- Shovel
- 12-volt DC transformer
- 12-volt DC light fixtures
- 12-2 lighting cable suitable for burying
- Outdoor-rated connectors and fittings
- Automatic timer

1

2

3

⇜ 5 ⇝

Fish and Plants

CREATING A WATER GARDEN OPENS UP A NEW WORLD FILLED with fascinating plants with growth habits that may be completely new to you. Some have gorgeous flowers; some have attractive, variegated, or intriguing foliage; and some have all—there are many appealing choices.

Water gardening also gives you an opportunity to keep fish. Fabulously colored, ever moving, surprisingly interactive, fish are the living jewels of a water garden. They're simple to keep, but pay off big, eliciting cries of delight from children and adults alike who spot them from under the cover of water lilies. Larger fish, especially the ornamental carp known as koi, can even be trained to eat out of your outstretched hand.

Water Quality for Fish and Plants

Plants have simple water quality needs while fish prefer water that is the correct pH and free from potentially harmful elements.

If your water feature contains no plants or fish, your primary water quality concern is simple: keeping algae at bay. If you want to include fish, you'll need to give some thought to water quality. While fish will tolerate many different types of water, for them to be in tip-top health, it's smart for you to take into account everything from chloramines to nitrogen levels.

The Right pH Levels

You may already be familiar with pH in your garden soil since some plants prefer acidic soil and some prefer alkaline. The pH level describes how alkaline (also called basic or hard) or how acidic the water is, measured on a 14-point scale.

With both soil and water, a pH of 7 is considered neutral. A pH higher than 7 is basic while levels below 7 are acidic.

Typical, healthy ponds have a pH range from 6 to 11. A pH of 8.2, for example, supports a plants and fish well, while a pH of 4 (which is acidic enough to dissolve nails) would obviously be a problem.

Test your water with a simple, inexpensive pH kit available at most garden centers or online. Then, as needed, adjust pH levels with special chemicals purchased through water garden suppliers, made specifically to correct water garden pH.

Chlorine and Chloramines

Chlorine is harmful to both fish and aquatic plants, and is present in nearly all city water. Luckily, it dissipates from water if you let the water sit for 5 to 7 days. Or you can add a special dechlorinator to remove chorine in minutes.

Chloramines, which can also be present in water supplies, are also of concern and can kill fish. Contact your local water supplier to ask if chloramines are present. If they are, treat the water with a chloramine remover before adding fish and whenever you add or replace more than 20 percent of the water.

Oxygen

Fish need well-oxygenated water to sustain life. That's why a fountain or waterfall, which constantly aerates the water, is so helpful. Plants also are a boon to oxygen levels in water, especially submerged plants, as they release oxygen from their foliage.

Water temperature affects oxygen levels. Water that becomes too warm quickly loses oxygen. So guarantee that it stays cool by designing your water garden so that it's large enough and deep enough that it doesn't quickly overheat in the sun. Also site your pool so it gets some shade, particularly in the afternoon. Add floating plants for additional shade in the water.

Nitrogen, Nitrates, Nitrites, and Ammonia

Even low levels of nitrogen and its related forms—nitrates, nitrites, and ammonia—can be toxic to fish.

A primary cause of high nitrogen levels is too many fish. Fish produce a lot of nitrogen-rich waste, so limit their size and numbers. Also use adequate filtering and clean the filters regularly. Include plenty of marginal plants and submerged plants since they filter and oxygenate the water.

Overfeeding fish also contributes to problems because uneaten food breaks down and produces nitrogen-related waste.

Signs of high levels of nitrogen include too much algae or fish dying.

If you have a concern about the nitrogen levels in you pond, purchase a test kit and test. If needed, treat with special water conditioners made specifically to control nitrogen levels, by cleaning the filters, and by changing out 10 to 20 percent of the water.

Different water kits test for different elements and are available at better-stocked garden centers, water garden specialty stores, or online.

The Wonderful World of Water Plants

If you've always been a "terrestrial gardener," you are in for a treat. The plants that enjoy life in water are an utterly fascinating group, with needs and growth habits quite different from other garden plants.

Water Garden Plant Tips

Water garden plants do more than just look good. All help purify and filter the water. They shade it and keep it cool. They compete with algae and, with your help, have the winning hand. Some also provide food and cover for fish and other garden wildlife.

Water garden plants fall into one of four groups:

- **Water lilies and lotuses** grow at the bottom of ponds, with long stems growing to the surface with large, flat pad-like leaves and gorgeous flowers on top. They serve most of the same functions as other water garden plants, but their show-stopping beauty, incredible flowers, and fragrance are what really earn them devotees.
- **Marginal plants** grow in shallow water. Also called bog plants, there are hundreds to choose from, depending on your tastes, climate, and their availability.
- **Submerged plants** grow mainly underwater. They are a good addition to a pool or pond to add oxygen to the water and provide cover for fish.
- **Floating plants** simply float on the water surface, their roots dangling below. They spread rapidly in warm weather and shade the pond, preventing algae growth and cooling the water for fish.

What Kind of Soil?

Most water garden plants do well in rich, heavy organic soil from your garden, or in compost mixed with garden soil. A little extra clay content is a plus, and some water gardeners like to add sand to allow water to better move through the soil. Regular potting soil is too light and will float away, but you can also purchase potting soil made specifically for aquatic plants.

Once a water garden plant is potted, top the soil with 1 to 2 inches of pea gravel or very small stones. This keeps the soil in place and also helps weight down the pot. It's a good idea to put a stone or two in the bottom of a water garden container to provide ballast to prevent them from tipping or drifting.

What Kind of Pots?

With most water garden plants, you can keep them in the same black plastic pots they're sold in at garden centers. The dark color helps them blend in with the water and black liner. The holes in the bottom are adequate for allowing water to pass through.

Water lilies usually need large, wider, and more shallow black plastic pots. Large marginal plants, such as taro, need pots about as large as a bushel basket—more like tubs.

Specialty water garden containers are a useful option. Most resemble plastic baskets and

Water garden plants do more than just look good. They also help balance the ecosystem of a pond.

are lined with a special black fabric-like liner or landscape fabric.

Where to Position the Pots?

It's not as important where the bottom of the pot rests as much as where the top is. Most water garden plants do best with the soil surface of the pot an inch or two below the water surface.

(Water lilies are the exception—they like deeper water. See page 124.)

When possible, design your water garden with a variety of depths to accommodate different plants (see page 74). You can also erect stands in the water on which to set plants. Black plastic crates are perfect for this job, but you can also use flat stones and bricks, as long as they're not crumbling.

How to Plant Water Garden Plants

Potting up aquatic plants is very similar to planting their land-locked cousins, but with a few twists.

1

Preparing the Pot

If you are using a special aquatic pot or other container with large openings, line it with a loose-weave fabric made specifically for that purpose, landscape fabric, or natural burlap. Put a stone or other weight in the bottom to serve as ballast to prevent tipping or drifting.

2

Adding Soil

Fill the pot partway with soil. Water well or set the container in a partly filled tub and let it soak. Wet down additional soil in a separate bucket to add later.

3

Positioning the Plant

If necessary, remove the plant from its current container by firmly knocking it out. Be gentle with some plants—water lilies and others can have quite brittle roots. Then position in the pot, and fill in with the additional wet soil. Pack it in gently but firmly. Leave space for the gravel on top.

4

Adding Gravel

Rinse off pea or other dark gravel. Add a layer 1 to 2 inches deep to keep soil in place even when the pot's underwater.

5

Positioning the Pot

Set the plant in the pond at the appropriate depth for that plant (check the label). Marginal plants usually need an inch or two of water over their soil surface. Submerged plants can be positioned with their crowns 1 to 2 feet deep. Water lilies do best when placed in more shallow water at first to allow the leaves to develop and are then placed in deeper water. (See page 74.)

Tools and Supplies

Plant

Pot

Soil from your garden or aquatic potting mix

Sand (optional)

Pea gravel

Good Idea!

The water garden plants you buy may already be in a black plastic pot. If the pot is large enough to accommodate future growth, there's no need to repot. Just rinse off the soil and plant to make sure there isn't any algae or duckweed hiding in there. Then top with some gravel, if needed, and put it in your water garden!

Water Lilies and Lotuses

These stars of the water garden show have been the inspiration for some homeowners to get into water gardening in the first place. They come in every color of the rainbow with flower forms so delightful they've been the inspiration for artwork and paintings for centuries.

All water lilies prefer at least six hours of direct, unfiltered light a day. They also fare best in still water—if a fountain is splashing them or a nearby waterfall is churning the water even more than slightly, they'll struggle.

There are two kinds of water lilies: hardy and tropical. Logically, gardeners in colder climates have more success with hardies, and gardeners with long, hot summers report spectacular results with tropicals. Even so, either or both can be grown well in most parts of North America, but you'll just have to take more pains to meet their needs.

There is a wide variety of water lilies and lotuses. When choosing one, consider size. Some water lilies are naturally small, spreading out their pads to cover an area only 4 to 6 feet wide, while others, given a chance, will become enormous, spreading up to 20 feet across. Stock your pool according to mature plant estimates.

In old-fashioned ponds, water lilies were planted directly in the mud at the bottom. Modern water gardeners plant them in pots that are wide and shallow to accommodate their spreading habit. Hardy water lilies, for example, need a pot about 16 inches across and 7 inches deep. Unlike marginal plants (see page 128), the larger types of water lilies thrive in deeper water, preferring their crowns to be 18 to 24 inches below the water's surface. Miniatures and other smaller types like more shallow depths.

When planting water lilies, first place them in a shallow portion of the pond to allow their stems to grow and elongate. After a few weeks, you can then place them in a deeper position.

Water lilies and lotuses are greedy feeders, so fertilize regularly. Use a fertilizer formulated for aquatic plants and follow label directions.

Depending on your climate and the type of water lily or lotus, you can save your water lilies each fall by cutting them back and setting them in the deep zone of your water garden, where it won't freeze. Devoted water gardeners in cold climates cut them back and bring them indoors, setting them in tubs of water under grow lights.

Water lilies need still water, so plant them away from waterfalls and fountains.

Hardy water lilies, such as this 'Marliacea Chromatella', thrive in cooler temperatures and are good choices for the northern half of the United States and the Pacific Northwest.

Hardy Water Lilies

Nymphaea species
Mature plant size: Spreads on the water's surface 2 to 12 feet, depending on the type
Hardy: Zones 4–10

A good choice for water gardens in the northern half or so of the United States, hardy water lilies are able to withstand colder temperature than tropical water lilies or lotuses. You can even overwinter them by putting them in a deep portion of a water feature, if you have one, where the water does not freeze.

Their flowers tend to be smaller and less showy than tropicals and usually have less fragrance. There are no night-blooming types. Flower colors are limited to white, pink, yellow, peach, and red, and bloom time spans spring through fall.

Tropical water lilies, such as this 'Queen of Siam', rise up above the water on taller stems than hardy water lilies.

Tropical Water Lilies

Nymphaea species
Mature plant size: Spread of 1 to 10 or more feet on the water surface, depending on the type
Hardy: Zones 10–11

Tropical water lilies are valued even more than hardy types for good reason: They tend to have more and larger flowers than the hardy type with a color range that truly does include every color of the rainbow, including the true black to true blues to rich purples that are almost non-existent in hardy types.

Tropicals are noted for their rich flower fragrance, which spreads through the air. Tropical water lilies come in two different types: day-bloomers and night-bloomers. Both have distinctive flowers that are held on stems regally above the water surface. And while nearly all tropical water lilies have a richer, heavier fragrance than the hardy types, the night-bloomers have the most intense scent of all.

Plant in spring only after the water temperature has warmed to 70° F. Plant tropical water lilies so their crowns are 4 to 12 inches below the water surface. They can't take cold water or frost, so either purchase new ones each year or overwinter them in tubs of water indoors under grow lights or in a greenhouse.

This lotus displays its classic seedpod, an added attraction of this exotic flower.

Lotus

Nelumbo species

Mature plant size: 12 to 60 inches high and wide, depending on the type
Hardy: Zones 5–11

Highly fragrant, exotic-looking lotus is the literal stuff of legends. It produces dramatic, huge lilypad-like leaves and incredible afternoon- or evening-blooming flowers up to a foot across.

Miniature or dwarf lotuses grow just 1 to 3 feet high with leaves that are just 2 to 3 inches across, yet they can produce flowers several inches across atop stems that can reach as much as 6 feet. The standard types grow 6 to 8 feet tall with leaves 18 inches to 3 feet in diameter.

Key to growing lotuses is extended warm— actually hot—temperatures, lots of sun, and ample fertilizer. They will grow in the short summers of most of the northern third of the United States and Pacific Northwest, but not as dramatically. Lotuses really need two or even three consecutive months of temperatures above 80 degrees F. Further, fussy lotuses dislike humidity. However, some lotuses are surprisingly hardy, surviving even Zone 5 winters with proper protection.

Lotuses are also for the patient water gardener. Most bloom in their second year, but may bloom the first year if they receive heavy fertilizing.

A lotus tuber looks a bit like a double banana, with one or two buds. The entire structure is extremely fragile and brittle. Handle with great care during planting. If the growing end is broken off, it's wise to just throw the whole thing away, sadly, as the remaining section will rot.

Lotuses need large but shallow containers, planted so the crowns are 2 to 12 inches below the surface. For standard types, choose a container at least 18 inches and up to 3 feet across and about half as deep. They prefer water up to their crown, but will tolerate as little as 2 to 3 inches of water if necessary.

Marginal Water Garden Plants

A marginal plant—sometimes called a bog plant—is one that in nature grows on the sides of a pond or in a damp area, hence the name. As in the wild, they look best on the perimeters of the water, helping integrate your pool into the landscape around it.

There are myriad interesting choices for marginal plants. Some, such as taro and variegated canna, reach 6 feet and have dramatic big foliage. Others have tall, thin, elegant profiles, such as papyrus. Still others have large, gorgeous flowers, such as yellow flag.

Marginals don't need deep water. Most are perfectly happy with "wet feet but dry ankles," meaning that they really only need an inch or two of water over their crown.

How to Grow

The basic need of a marginal is lots of water, and since they're in a water feature, that need is easily met! Otherwise these plants as a group require little work to maintain. Some are rampant growers, which can be a problem on land. But in the water garden, in pots, they are contained. Also, pots allow you to move them around to put them in just the right site for best growth and visual advantage.

Fertilizing marginal plants is usually not necessary since they get nitrogen from the water, though some do better with fertilizing. Marginals of tropical origin (those hardy only to Zones 9 or 10) should not be placed in water colder than 70 degrees F, and they won't tolerate frost, so exercise caution in setting out plants in early spring.

Tips on Tipping

Because of the upright growth habit of many marginals, they are more apt to topple in a breeze or during a summer storm than their lower-growing, floating-leaf companions. Pond visitors, including pest ones like raccoons, may also knock them over. When this happens, right them as soon as possible and replace the gravel layer on their soil surface, if need be.

You can prevent toppling in the first place by adding ballast, such as a stone or brick, to the bottom of the pot, at planting time. Or place in dark colored tubs or crates, or surround with boulders to hold in place.

Best for Bogs

Marginal plants also do well in "bogs," special planting beds that are lined so that they drain very slowly or not at all. Bog beds mimic the swamps and marshy low spots that water-loving marginals love. Fill the planting bed with rich, dark soil—adding some sphagnum peat moss also is helpful.

Bog beds can be created as completely separate from a water garden, but you can also create a bog "edge" that allows water to flow into the bog bed but does not allow soil to flow out into the water garden. These connected bog planting pockets can be placed alongside a pond or stream or waterfall.

Arrowhead
Sagittaria latifolia
Mature plant size: 2–4 feet high and wide
Hardy: Zones 4 or 5–10

Arrowhead grows easily, flowers readily, and looks nice with other water-garden plants, including water lilies. The bright green, three-pointed leaves are arrowhead-shaped; the perky little three-petaled flowers are carried on stalks among them.

This plant grows from small tubers, and its pot may be submerged in as little as an inch of water and perhaps as much as a foot. Cover the potted plant's surface with gravel to prevent the soil from drifting into the pool and to discourage ducks and other waterfowl that relish the tasty tubers.

The awl-leaved arrowhead, *Sagittaria subulata*, has some larger submerged leaves and smaller floating leaves. Japanese arrowhead, *Sagittaria sagittifolia*, has purple-marked flowers and can be invasive; its cultivar 'Flore Pleno' is said to be less aggressive and has huge white pom-pom flowers. Aztec or giant arrowhead, *Sagittaria montevidensis*, is treasured for its beautiful red-accented, pure-white flowers and is hardy in Zones 8–10.

This versatile plant also can be brought indoors for a houseplant, as long as you keep it well watered.

Canna
Canna × *generalis*
Mature plant size: 2–8 feet high × 1–3 feet wide
Hardy: Zones 6–10

For tropical pizzazz in your water garden, water-loving cannas deliver. They are quite tall and have large, banana leaf-like leaves. The sensational blossoms appear starting in midsummer and come in a range of bright colors and bicolors, primarily red, hot pink, orange, and yellow. Canna with reddish, bronze, striped, or variegated leaves are assets even when the plants are not blooming.

Give these showy plants full sun and large pots (for their roots and also for stability). They also benefit from regular fertilizing. As for placement, because they are so tall and large, give them a background position, a corner, or a spot out in the center—anywhere where they can be well admired without blocking the view of lower-growers. Cannas kept in the lower depths of a pond have even proven to be hardy as far north as Zone 6. Tubers can be allowed to dry and saved over the winter in regions where cannas are not hardy.

Creeping Jenny, Moneywort

Lysimachia nummularia
Mature plant size: 1–2 inches high × 3 feet wide
Hardy: Zones 3–8

Growing in damp ground, the long trailing stems of this handsome groundcover can become a nuisance, spreading almost invasively. In a water garden, confined to a pot, however, creeping Jenny is manageable and a delight. The coin-shaped leaves are small and float on the surface, wending their way among water lilies or forming a skirt at the base of more vertical growers. Numerous little yellow, cup-shaped flowers appear in June or so, rising a bit above the leaves.

Place pots of creeping Jenny in shallow water, no more than 3 inches deep. If growth gets too vigorous, remove unwanted stems at the crown.

This is a wonderful bog plant as long as it is well contained and can't spread easily into surrounding soil. Creeping Jenny is also nice trailing over the side of a container garden or cascading downward along a waterfall. This plant spreads rapidly so space generously, 18 inches or more apart.

Iris

Iris species and hybrids
Mature plant size: 1–3 feet high × 1–2 feet wide
Hardy: Zones 4–9, in most cases

Irises have handsome, strap-like or spear-shaped foliage, sometimes with variegated stripes. Irises generally are untroubled by nibbling pests, which helps them remain attractive long after the flowers fade in late spring. Irises are good filter plants—they take nutrients from the water and contribute to keeping it clear.

Immerse potted iris plants in 1-gallon pots in shallow water, generally 6 inches deep or less. Full sun is best, but some will do well in light shade.

Land-locked types of iris, interestingly, need dry conditions and good drainage. But several types love boggy, wet conditions. Yellow flag (*Iris pseudocaorus*) is a brilliant golden classic that will grow in large colonies along the edges of ponds and streams. It also does well in pots set into water gardens.

All the Louisiana irises are suitable for water displays. Also try pale blue *Iris versicolor* and *Iris virginica* and the rusty-colored copper iris (*Iris fulva*). Also consider Siberian iris (*Iris sibirica*), Japanese iris (*Iris ensata*, also known as *Iris kaempferi*), and *Iris laevigata*.

Papyrus, Umbrella Palm

Cyperus species and cultivars
Mature plant size: Varies
Hardy: Zones 8–10

Papyrus is a large group of plants, with plenty of variety in size and height. Their green leaves are stiff and triangular, and the plant is vertical and upright. Tufts of brownish flowers surrounded by what are technically whorls of spiked foliage in greenish hues add heft.

The biggest one—reaching a towering 6 feet or more—is the Egyptian paper reed, *Cyperus papyrus*, once used in paper-making. At the other end of the scale is the dwarf papyrus, *Cyperus haspan*, at a mere 30 inches. In between is the ever-popular umbrella palm, *Cyperus alternifolius*, which gets to about 3 to 5 feet. All aid in water clarity. Papyrus can also be overwintered indoors as a houseplant as long as you keep it well watered.

An especially desirable variation is *Cyperus alternifolius* 'Variegatus', which is shorter and has lengthwise white stripes. A nice, compact edition is *Cyperus involucratus* 'Nanus', which stays about 2 feet high.

Taro, Elephant's Ear

Colocasia esculenta
Mature plant size: 2–6 feet high × 2–4 feet wide
Hardy: Zones 9–11

Spectacular tropical foliage plants, taros have big heart-shaped leaves reaching 3 or more feet. These shed water the way lotus leaves do, and may be marked with purple or cranberry red or have contrasting margins or veins. They also do well in light to medium shade.

Taro plants grow from a tuber. Plant each one several inches deep in an ample-sized pot, without covering the growing tip. Set it in moist soil or up to 6 inches of water. Fertilizing prompts more lush growth.

In Zones 8 and colder, treat it like a houseplant over the winter. Or dry just the tuber and stored it in a cool place where temperatures do not dip to freezing.

The very popular 'Black Magic' has dark purple, nearly black, leaves and stems. 'Illustris' has gorgeous blue-black leaves and thick green veining and hits about 3 feet in height.

Submerged Plants

Submerged plants grow under the water, with perhaps just a bit of their foliage drifting on top. They're a good way to keep the water clear and aerated.

Submerged plants sometimes are also called oxygenators, and that summarizes their primary role in a water garden. These vital underwater plants may not be obvious to the casual admirer of your water garden, but they are the unsung heroes. During daytime hours when they photosynthesize, they produce oxygen. This additional oxygen is a boon to fish. Also, their trailing foliage and roots provide a place for fish to hide from predators as well as an ideal place to spawn.

Nature's Own Water Filters

Submerged plants also help keep the pool water clear by filtering out nutrients that would otherwise remain in the water and encourage algae growth.

Most submerged plants are grassy-looking plants that aren't especially attractive, but then again, they aren't readily visible either, so it's not a worry. They're available from any water-garden or aquarium supplier.

How many submerged plants to include? One formula is to add 1 submerged plant for every 4 square feet of surface area. But experiment to find out what works best for your water garden.

Most submerged plants do well when in full sun. Most prefer that their crown—the place where the roots meet the stems—is at least a foot or so deep so that most of the foliage is in the water and buoyed upward. Check the label to find optimal conditions for your plant.

Flowers as Well as Foliage

A few submerged plants flower as well, but they are grown almost exclusively for their foliage and ability to improve water quality.

It may be tempting in a small water garden to put soil in the bottom of the pond and grow submerged plants the way it happens in nature. But this method often makes for muddy water. Also, some of these plants can be aggressive and, if they take hold, will overrun a pool or pond.

Not Quite Submerged

In all but the deepest water gardens, most submerged plants grow to the surface of the water and float somewhat along the surface of the water. Some gardeners think this looks messy; others like it because it adds interest and another layer of greenery and flowering to their water gardens. If you don't care for this effect, it's easy enough to occasionally cut back your submerged plants by about half throughout the growing season.

Parrot's Feather
Myriophyllum aquaticum
Mature plant size: ½–2+ feet high and wide
Hardy: Zones 6–11

Bright green, unbranched stems are lined with feathery whorls of leaves (up to 3 inches in diameter!). There is a dwarf, red-stemmed variety, *Myriophyllum proserpinacoides*, which is gaining popularity because its growth is more compact and manageable. Another compact type is *Myriophyllum heterophyllum*.

A handsome, vigorous plant, parrot's feather is not content to remain underwater and may poke its head out or even trail over your display's edges (or the rim of its container, if you grow it in one). It shelters baby fish, and also does well in deep water pools, so plant it two feet or deeper. In any event, though, you must keep after it, tearing out excess growth so it doesn't overwhelm small pools or entire sections of larger pools.

Parrot's feather is invasive and is banned in Alabama, Connecticut, Maine, Massachusetts, Vermont, and Washington.

Hornwort
Ceratophyllum demersum
Mature plant size: 1–2 feet high, trailing
Hardy: Zones 6–10

You may have seen this one in aquariums (including plastic versions), and it makes a fine transition to an outdoor water garden.

Once you drop it in the pool, it remains underwater, neither floating on the surface nor sinking right to the bottom—oddly enough, it can exist without developing any roots, though in some situations it will loosely anchor itself to the bottom of a pond. During winter, it drops down to lower depths. It can be used in still or moving water, so it would work in ponds with fountains.

Fish often seek shelter in hornwort's whorls of thin, needle-like, branched foliage, or even spawn within its bounds. Koi tend not to bother it. It makes excellent cover when planted in groups for tiny newly hatched fish to hide in from overhead predators and larger fish that might eat them.

Floating Plants

If you've never planted a floating plant before, you're in for a treat: Just drop it in and step back!

Floating plants are excellent additions to many water gardens because they shade the water and absorb nutrients, which retard algae growth, keep the water cooler for fish, and are simply a pretty addition.

But use caution; they should cover about two-thirds and not the entire pond. Plant floating plants in spring, after all danger of frost has passed in your region.

Once temperatures warm, they spread rapidly. In fact, in a number of southern states, these floating plants are banned or classified as noxious weeds. If they escape into creeks, rivers, or large ponds, they often become invasive, choking out native plants.

With tiny floating plants such as fairy moss and duckweed, you need to be especially careful. If the garden center where you purchased a plant has either of these plants in the water, and you don't want it in your water feature, rinse the plant thoroughly to remove any hidden bits that are hitching a ride on the plant you've purchased.

If you like fairy moss, *Azolla filiculoides,* it's hardy to Zones 5–10, and matures to about ⅜ inch high. It's really an aquatic fern, with two-lobed fuzzy leaves on short stems. It forms small colonies from mid- to late spring. It's a rampant grower, good for when you need quick surface coverage, but it needs to be thinned and can be invasive. Duckweed, *Lemna minor* (hardy to Zones 3–11), is sometimes called the world's smallest plant. Each plant has roots hanging below its lime green, oval-shaped leaves. This allows the plant to float freely, taking up whatever nutrition it needs directly from the water. It tends to hitchhike on other water plants. If it reproduces too vigorously, just discard handfuls into your compost pile. Goldfish and koi like to nibble it.

As summer progresses, thin your floating plants if they start to completely cover the pond and create a visual effect you don't care for. Just take a rake or other long-handled tool and pull them out, and toss on the compost pile.

In winter, if your region gets frost, floating plants will die back. Simply pull them out and compost them. In cold regions of the country, if you are keeping fish in an aquarium, you might want to add a few of these to overwinter. If you have a grow light, you can also put a few in a bucket until spring. Otherwise, purchase new floating plants in spring.

Water Hyacinth

Eichhornia crassipes
Mature plant size: 6–12 inches high and wide
Hardy: Zones 8–11

This plant is both a beauty and a beast. It has glossy green leaves and spikes of lovely purple or lavender (occasionally white) flowers that have been likened to floating orchids. They are undeniably pretty among water lilies of compatible hues, and the plant contributes to valuable water surface coverage. The spongy stems are inflated, enabling the plant to float while feathery roots trail below. Fish often spawn there. The roots also take up nutrients out of the water so efficiently that some municipalities have used this plant to assist in water purification.

In the wild, however, water hyacinth is an unwelcome pest. Don't dispose of plants in bodies of water. If desired, overwinter in a warm acquarium, or simply buy new in spring.

Water hyacinth is banned in Arizona, and considered a noxious weed in Alabama, California, Connecticut, Florida, South Carolina, and Texas.

Water Lettuce

Pistia stratiotes
Mature plant size: 4 inches high × 8 inches wide
Hardy: Zones: 8–11

The handsome textured leaves of water lettuce invite touching. They are soft, velvety, and shed droplets of water in a beautiful pattern when splashed. The rosettes float on the water surface, forming dense colonies over time. Fish spawn in the long, dangling roots that trail below.

Water lettuce can be sensitive to too much direct sun, which can turn the leaves yellow or have burnt brown edges. It's best used in spots that don't receive direct sun all day.

Set out in water in spring after all danger of frost has passed. In cool spring temperatures, water lettuce won't do much. But once the water warms up, it spreads rapidly.

Water lettuce can be invasive, so keep it away from natural bodies of water. It is banned in Connecticut and Florida, and classified as a noxious weed in Alabama, South Carolina, and Texas.

Water Garden Fish

Darting fish are a fascinating, fun sight in the water garden. They're practical as well, playing an important part in a pond's ecological balance.

Some homeowners install a pond in their backyard specifically so that they can enjoy fish and other aquatic creatures. Fish in a water feature make it seem more alive and more enchanting. Koi will actually come and eat from your hand and can be trained to do simple tricks. Water features, too, can host other creatures that lend to their interest and diversity, including snails, frogs, toads, butterflies, dragonflies, turtles, birds, and more.

Fish have their role in the overall ecosystem of a pond. They can be useful scavengers, nibbling algae and organic debris, including decaying plant stems and foliage. They eat pest insects, particularly mosquito larvae. Last but not least, the carbon dioxide produced by their respiration is immediately available to your plants.

How Many Fish?

If you put too many fish in your water feature, conditions will become unhealthy due to too much fish waste and too little oxygen. The number of fish you add depends on how large your water feature is, how much filtration you have, and how many plants. A conservative rule of thumb is 1 inch of fish for every 10 gallons of water.

Another rule of thumb, which allows for squeezing in more fish, recommends 1 inch of fish for each 6 to 12 square inches of water surface. For koi, however, double the amount of water surface required.

Aeration also plays a role. If you have a small fountain in your pond, you can have a two or three more fish than if you didn't. If you have a waterfall, which aerates the water substantially, you can have as many as double the amount of fish as you could without a waterfall.

A Good Environment for Fish

If fish are important to you, design your water feature large enough to accommodate the size and number of fish you want. If you live in a colder climate in the northern two-thirds of the United States, you will need to make some decisions about over-wintering your livestock. This is a complicated issue that you should discuss with the fish seller or other water gardeners in your area.

Different fish also prefer different depths. Koi need space to swim vertically, and need at least 2 feet of depth but they are happiest with 5 feet. In comparison, orfes spend most of their time in the upper regions of a pond and are content with very shallow water.

Filtration and aeration are important in features with fish, but be aware that fountains and filtration in a small pond can produce too much churn for fish. Tiny fish can get caught in even modest-sized mechanical filters and a waterfall or fountain may require fish to fight a current more than you would imagine.

Koi are definitely the king of water garden fish. They come in a connoisseur's array of colors and markings and can grow more than 3 feet long in optimal conditions.

Water quality is also critical for fish. (See pages 118–119.) Take measures to make sure the pH and other chemical levels of your water are suitable for fish.

In the southern third of the United States, fish do better with some afternoon shade from trees or water garden plants in order to keep water cool. Choose fish partly according to their temperature tolerances. Some fish can tolerate water just above freezing while others are fine in water temperatures as high as 95°F. On the other hand, very cold water can kill some fish while very warm water can kill others.

Choosing Fish

The array of fish readily available today is amazing. Visit your local pet store or aquatic shop to see the different types. You can spend anything from a few dollars on a common goldfish to hundreds of dollars on a choice koi specimen.

When buying fish, choose those that are young, preferably not more than 3 or 4 inches so they'll adapt more easily to their new home. They should have bright eyes and be active with no damaged or missing scales or fins.

It's best to choose fish of the same size since small fish less than 3 inches long can be eaten by larger fish. Also, when purchasing, ask which fish types get along (or don't) with other types of fish.

Koi

These large, brightly colored carp relatives are very popular, and no wonder—they're beautiful and fascinating. They can even be trained to come to the edges of your pond and eat fish snacks right out of your hand. So tame and intelligent are these fish that some people give them names and consider them pets.

They are classified by color, pattern, and scale type into more than a dozen major varieties. Markings include red, orange, white, black, yellow, brown, and blue.

Since koi grow big, as long as 3 feet, and swim both vertically and horizontally, they do best in a large pool 3 to 5 feet deep, though in mild climates in the lower third of the country they can survive in pools as shallow as 2 feet. However, water for koi needs to be cool. They prefer temperatures of 39°F to 78°F.

Hardy Goldfish

Hardy goldfish offer a wide variety of easy-care choices for the water garden enthusiast. If you're a beginner, you'd be wise to start off with the most inexpensive, such as goldfish, comets, or shubunkins, before investing in more expensive ones.

With inexpensive fish, you can discover with minimal financial loss if there are herons or other hungry predatory birds in your neighborhood. You'll learn how much food and how

Koi are prized by water gardeners for their size, markings, and intelligence. They can even be trained and some owners swear they have personalities.

Sarasa comets and shubunkins are two common types of hardy goldfish that work well in outdoor water features.

much waste a certain number of fish generates and can adjust the population accordingly. Also, pricier, more exotic fish tend to be less tough, that is, not as cold-hardy and perhaps in need of more highly filtered water than the cheap ones.

Goldfish are easily the most commonly kept fish. These fancy cousins of the common carp are available in a number of different types, such as black moors, comets, fantails, lionheads, orandas, ryukin, shubunkin, and others. Most goldfish live for a few years in a pond situation, but some can live up to 12 years.

More hardy types of goldfish can survive a winter outdoors even in cold climates as long as the water is kept open and they have an ice-free deep zone to retreat to. These include the common goldfish, comets, and shubunkins. Common goldfish, especially, are easy to keep and will tolerate more temperature extremes as well as poorer-quality water with less oxygen. Most hardy goldfish can tolerate temperatures just above freezing to 85°F to 95°F, though not for very long at either extreme.

Less hardy goldfish cannot survive well in temperatures below 40°F. They can tolerate temperatures as high as 80°F or so, but do best in water temperatures closer to 60°F and 70°F. They include fantails, veiltails, lionheads, and black moors. In fall, they need to be brought indoors to overwinter in aquariums.

Tropical Fish in a Water Garden

Some pond enthusiasts like to put tropical fish—the kind usually reserved for aquariums indoors—in water features. This can be done as long as the weather is warm enough. Most tropical fish don't like water temperatures below 70° F, which means air temperatures that aren't dipping at night below what your house might be like—65° F degrees or so. For the northern two-thirds of the country, that means tropical fish must spend colder parts of the year indoors in an aquarium.

Care and Feeding of Water Garden Fish

Some fish, such as koi, are surprisingly long-lived. Take care of them well and
they may live as many as 50 years—perhaps longer than you!

Add fish to a pond in late winter or spring when the water temperature has reached around 50°F, roughly your area's average last frost date. Add them only after you are sure your pond is chlorine- or chloramines-free.

When bringing fish home, keep them at room temperature (don't leave them in the car!) and don't keep the fish in the bag for more than an hour or two.

Acclimate the fish to the pool by floating the bag in the water for 15 or 20 minutes before releasing them. This allows them to gradually adjust their body temperatures—otherwise, they may die from temperature shock. After putting the fish in the pond, don't feed them for 3 to 4 days.

If you already have other fish, as a safeguard, when introducing fish to a pond with other fish, you may want to treat them with special fish salts to ensure that they are disease- and parasite-free so they don't spread any problems to other fish.

How to Feed Fish

In a pond with plants, it's easy to overfeed fish. Some may be fine without any feedings from you at all, instead eating plant roots, algae, and mosquito larvae.

Do check once or twice a week, however. Sprinkle a bit of food on the water. If the fish are not ravenous and do not eat the food immediately, they have plenty of food already. If they do eat well, do not give them more than they can eat in five minutes. Overfeeding contributes to waste in the water and will cloud water and create other quality problems.

Provide Shelter

Fish use shelter from plants and structures for protection from predators or as a spawning area or as protection from a current created by a fountain.

Underwater plants, floating plants, and marginal plants all create shelter. In the spring, before these plants are able to get very large, you may want to provide shelter by placing large clay or plastic pots on their side in the water. Try a flat stone propped up on other stones, or try a length of a large plastic or ceramic pipe as wide as a foot or more in diameter. For information on overwintering fish in cold climates, see page 136.

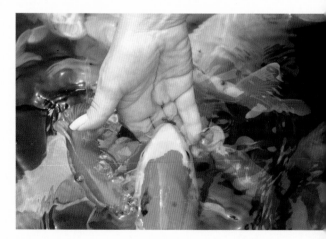

Koi often can be trained to eat right from your hand.

Other Water Creatures

A variety of water-loving animals besides fish, whether introduced by you or appearing on their own, can make important contributions to your pond's ecology.

When you create even a small water feature, it will attract animals and insects of all sorts. Some will be welcome, such as songbirds flitting in fountains or sipping from the edge. Butterflies like sipping salts from stones and shallow puddles. Dragonflies fly about.

Others will be less welcome. Raccoons may try to make a midnight snack of your fish. The neighbor's golden retriever may decide your pond is the perfect place for a cooling splash. Even blue herons, prized by some bird watchers, are not appreciated by homeowners whose expensive fish become a snack for these elegant birds.

Snails

Scavengers such as snails also are attracted to water gardens. They are little unsung heroes. Not only do they eat algae, but they also consume decaying plant tissue and other pool debris.

The most common choice is freshwater snails, available from water-garden suppliers and pet stores that supply aquarium hobbyists. You may also wish to add freshwater clams or freshwater mussels. Make sure you are buying ones that don't eat plants! The general formula for such scavengers is 1 or 2 per square foot of surface area.

Frogs and Toads

If frogs and toads appear in your water garden long enough to lay eggs, you'll welcome the tadpoles . . . in moderate numbers. These little creatures tend to eat a lot of insects. Children are fascinated by watching their rapid development.

The sounds frogs and toads make are delightful, filling a summer day's evening air. It sparks memories of exploring ponds and creeks for adults and can create a whole new set of memories for youngsters.

Turtles are one of the many types of animals that will be attracted to a water source in your backyard.

⇒ 6 ⇐

Maintaining Your Water Feature

*T*AKING CARE OF A WATER GARDEN DURING THE HEIGHT OF THE growing season is not much different from attending to other parts of your garden. You'll add water, fertilize, prune, ward off pests, and occasionally divide and repot. You'll also be keeping an eye on water quality, rinsing out filters, and making sure algae doesn't get an upper hand. But overall, water gardening is some of the lowest maintenance gardening around. You can leave for a weekend (or a couple of weeks) and rest assured that your water feature can pretty much take care of itself.

Coping with Algae

Keeping water clear and sparkling is the goal of every water gardener.
To do that, you'll need to arm yourself with tools and tips for keeping algae at bay.

Every water garden should have a little algae—it's a normal part of a balanced pond system. The trick is to keep it minimalized so water isn't cloudy and string algae doesn't get out of hand.

Types of Algae

There are two main types of algae that plague ponds.

Suspended algae is what makes water green. It usually occurs in the spring when the pond is first "waking up" and temperatures begin to rise. This is often called an algae bloom. Typically, this clears up in a week or two as beneficial bacteria also become active and water garden plants start growing and eliminating (eating) some of the nutrients in the water from the algae. Algae can become a problem later in the season as well, but spring is usually the time it's most prevalent.

String algae, also called filamentous algae, forms stringy chains or mats on rocks, plants, waterfalls, and other surfaces. It's a problem all growing season long. Sun, lots of fish producing waste, and lack of filtering plants in a pond all contribute.

Preventing Algae

Having a pond in ecological balance (see pages 16–17) is key to preventing algae. Keep nitrogen levels low by limiting fish and including lots of filtering plants so the algae will be starved out.

Including plenty of rocks and gravel in a water feature also helps. Bacteria colonize in the nooks between rocks and on rock surfaces.

These good bacteria also filter the water to prevent algae growth.

Floating plants keep algae at bay. These shade the water, depriving algae of sunlight. Like other plants, they also take up nitrogen from the water so algae can't.

Filtration (see page 58) is also critical. Mechanical filters such as skimmers catch debris before it can start to break down in the water, adding nitrogen. Biological filters contribute valuable bacteria that fight algae.

Treating Algae

One way to deal with string algae is to simply pull it out. You can use your hand or a narrow shrub rake or other tool.

As a last resort, you can also use various chemicals and additives to control algae in your water feature. There are a number of algaecides on the market. If you have fish and plants, choose one that specifies it is plant- and fish-safe. Most come in various liquid or granular forms. Read labels carefully and follow them *exactly*. Putting in too little is ineffective; putting in too much can harm fish and plants. Repeat applications as specified and as necessary.

You can also control algae by adding beneficial bacteria, which will break down nitrogen in the water, making it more difficult for algae to thrive.

Also, if you don't have any floating plants, consider adding them. They're excellent in controlling floating algae.

Use your hand, a rake, or even a toilet brush (used solely for this purpose!) to pull out string algae from your water feature.

Maintaining Filters

Filters are almost like vacuums, collecting debris, algae, and other unwanted particles from your garden. And just as with a vacuum, you need to empty them regularly or they won't function well.

How Often to Clean a Filter

Every filter needs to be cleaned out at least once in a while. How often depends on the type of filter, the size of the pond, the amount of algae and debris, and the time of year.

It's critical to keep filters clean. If the filter in any water garden filters a pump, a severely clogged filter can result in a burned-out pump.

You might need to clean a mat filter more often in the spring, after an algae bloom, when it gets clogged with algae. A skimmer may need to be emptied only every couple of weeks in spring and summer, but then almost daily in autumn to get rid of falling leaves.

When you first install your water feature, check the filter every two or three days. You'll soon be able to determine how often you need to clean it out to keep water flowing through it unimpeded.

Clean most filters simply by turning them or the attached pump off (unplugging is ideal for safety's sake). Then take the mat or bag or whatever section of the filter over to a garden hose and blast out visible particles. No need to get them perfectly clean—there are helpful bacteria in there too.

Methods for Cleaning Filters

How you clean the filter also depends on the type. With a skimmer (see page 60), simply lift out the debris basket and dump the leaves, twigs, and other debris into a compost heap or garbage can.

Many filters have fibrous mats to filter particles. With these, remove the mat and blast it from all directions with a garden hose to dislodge particles. Many filter mats are white, but don't worry if they're gray or discolored. Most are designed to last two or more years. Replace them only once they begin to tear or fall apart.

Biological filters usually don't need to be cleaned more than once a year. Cleaning them, especially with chlorinated tap water, can reduce or kill the beneficial bacteria key to these filters. If bioballs or other biological filter parts are becoming caked or clogged with debris, take a bucket or two of water from the water features and use that to rinse them out.

Replace the filter exactly the way you found it. With multiple filter mats, replace them so they are in the exact order in which you removed them. If there are slots or holes for discharge pipes of pumps and electrical cords to fit through, make sure they are correctly aligned.

This box filter holds the water feature's pump, so it's especially critical that it's cleaned regularly or the pump could clog and the motor would burn out.

Caring for Water Garden Plants

Water garden plants, as a group, need fairly little fussing over. Still, a bit of basic care will go a long way toward keeping them lush and healthy.

Increasingly, you can purchase water garden plants at most regular garden centers. But for the best selection, you may want to seek out a water garden specialty store or even buy plants online, though water garden plants don't always weather the trip well.

Fertilizing and More

Once your plants are in their pots (see page 120 for instructions), they may need fertilizing. Most marginal plants do fine with the nitrogen available in the water. But water lilies and lotuses are heavy feeders and benefit from regular fertilizing with special aquatic fertilizer, which usually comes in pellet form.

Other than that, during the growing season, most water garden plants need very little care. It's a good idea to trim off spent, damaged, or yellowing foliage, as well as dead flower heads.

Protecting Plants from Fish and Wind

Large fish, especially rambunctious koi, can do a surprising amount of damage to plants. If it's practical to do so, you can avoid fish damage by raising the pot so the rim of it is just 1 or 2 inches below water level. This makes it more difficult for fish to attack a plant's crown and stems.

It's also a good idea to secure pots by surrounding them with small boulders to prevent currents, large fish, or wind (for those tall plants in containers) from knocking them over.

Some water garden plants need regular fertilizing with a special aquatic plant fertilizer to achieve their best growth.

Winter Care in Severe Climates

Many gardeners with small water gardens just pitch their plants in fall and buy new ones in spring. But if you have many plants or valuable plants, you'll want to save them over the winter.

In climates where winter temperatures can plunge to 10, 20, or even 30 degrees below freezing, you need to take special steps to overwinter plants.

If your pond is large enough and deep enough for your part of the country (see page 73), cut back the plants and set them into the deep zone until spring.

Some plants, such as taros, umbrella palms, and arrowheads, are fine to bring indoors as regular houseplants, as long as you keep them well watered. Still others, such as water lilies, will do okay if you bring them indoors and put them in tubs, covered up to their crowns, under a grow light.

Water Garden Diseases

Most water garden plants are surprisingly disease-resistant. However, they will indeed experience insect, fungal diseases, and rot if you don't provide the following:

- A pot that is large enough. Roots packed in too tightly are susceptible to rot.

- Space between plants. Poor circulation encourages fungal problems.

- Adequate sun. Plants that struggle for light become weakened and prone to disease and insect attacks. Most water garden plants need at least 6 to 8 hours of direct, unfiltered sun.

- Trim off spent foliage. It encourages plants to send out strong, new growth. Yellowing and dead foliage attracts insects and disease.

- Set the plants out at the proper time in spring. Plants set out too early are damaged and weakened by cold, and prone to problems.

- Set the plants at the proper depth. Plants set too deep in the pond may decay.

- Make sure the pH of your garden is in the optimum range (see page 118).

Caring for Fish

Water garden fish are some of the lowest maintenance pets around.
With a good pond setup, they're almost carefree.

Feeding

Some fish can live with almost no additional feeding in a pond situation, providing there are plenty of plant materials and mosquitoes and insects to feed upon.

However, especially in the spring and fall, check on fishes' needs. Koi, especially, are hungry fish and need regular feeding. To determine how much food your fish need, never give them more than they can hungrily devour in five minutes. If food is left floating in the water, feed them less food, less often. Use a fish food made specifically for your kind of fish.

Keep fish handling to a minimum. It stresses fish and can even result in their death.

Shelter and Predators

Raccoons and herons—even the neighborhood cat—may find your fish a tasty treat. Protect fish by providing shelter in the form of floating and underwater plants. Or create a little underwater bunker for fish by placing a black plastic bucket on its side, anchored with rocks. Lengths of black plastic or ceramic pipe 1 to 2 feet across work well for larger fish. You can also arrange stones and overhangs with stone edging for shelter.

If predators are a consistent problem, put special pond or other netting over the water feature to block them out.

Winter Care

In areas with cold winters, you can keep koi and hardy goldfish in a pond all winter long. These fish can tolerate cold water temperatures if there's a deep zone in the pond where water won't freeze. Fish also need an open spot in the ice to allow oxygen and other gases to escape. Achieve this with a floating electric de-icer. Or install a recirculating pump on the highest shelf of your pond.

Don't feed fish after water temperatures dip below 50°F. Their systems slow down in very cold water and they go into a state almost of dormancy.

If necessary, consider bringing fish indoors. You can set up an aquarium in your home, or even just a large plastic bin. Be sure to have adequate aeration and filtration, and to feed them as needed. Even then, however, the transition and conditions tend to stress them.

Diseases

If all of your fishes' needs are met and they aren't overcrowded, fish diseases should be minimal. However, like any animal, pond fish can be prone to diseases—ulcers, parasites, and fungi.

If these occur, check out the several medications available for water garden fish and use exactly according to the label.

You can also use preventative medications, such as pond salts. Pond salts are added to the water to replace fish's natural electrolytes. You can use pond salts in any situation where fish might need a boost, as when they are first introduced to a pond or have been removed and are stressed, or if there's been an outbreak of disease in a pond and you want to protect the other fish.

Feeding Koi

Koi are especially heavy feeders. Feed them special koi pellets that are available and, if you desire, supplement their diet with treats like lettuce and cabbage or even small pieces of watermelon. Smaller and younger koi eat at least once a day, while large ones need breakfast, lunch, and dinner. Keep koi well fed, or they may nibble on your water plants!

Seasonal Maintenance: Spring Care

Spring is when you'll do the majority of work on your water feature, starting with a good cleanup.

As temperatures rise in late winter and early spring, determine if your water feature needs a complete cleaning or just a bit of tidying up. If there is a layer of sludge at the bottom, or the water is dark, it's probably time to do a full clean.

Perform your spring pond cleaning in early spring before plants awaken completely from their winter dormancy—about the time flowering trees are just start to bud but aren't flowering yet.

Tools and Supplies

- For larger water features, a sump or clean-out pump
- A garden hose with a high-pressure nozzle, or a power washer
- Hand-shears
- A wading pool, tub, or other container to hold fish and water animals
- A fish net
- Buckets, tubs, or a wheelbarrow to collect leaves and debris
- Pond chemicals and additives, as needed (see page 118) to remove chlorine and other harmful elements

Drain the Water Feature

Bail out water from a small feature. For larger features, place the clean-out pump in the deepest point of the pond. Drain onto the surrounding landscape, making sure not to flood areas and do damage. Put some of the water in containers to hold the fish. Once the water level is low enough to catch them easily, net the fish. Put them in the holding container in the shade to keep them cool and don't keep them in the holding container for more than a few hours.

If you've overwintered any plants under-water, remove them now.

Start Cleaning

Rinse the inside of the pond. You can also use a pressure washer to help remove debris from the rocks and gravel. Scrub away some, but not all, of the algae. You want to preserve some to preserve the balance of the pond, so limit removal. For pond about 11 by 16 feet, the scrubbing should take only 15 minutes or so.

Use a gentle water spray on rocks and gravel. Start at the top and work your way down to the bottom. Periodically turn the clean-out pump on to remove the dirty water. Stop pumping once the water at the bottom starts to look clear.

Also clean filters.

3

Add Water and Fish

Refill the pond, adding de-chlorinators and other water conditioners to the water so it's safe for fish.

After adding the other pond conditioners, add purchased beneficial bacteria to the water to restart their colonization.

Set up pumps, fountains, and filters and get them running, which will further improve water quality.

Fill a bucket with water from the holding container of fish. Net the fish and put them in the bucket. Set the bucket in the clean water for 15 to 20 minutes to allow water temperature to adjust to that of the pond, periodically splashing some pond water into the bucket. When the temperature of the pond and the bucket water are the same, gently release the fish into the newly cleaned pond.

With overwintered plants, trim off dead or damaged foliage. Set them at their appropriate water depth for the growing season, depending on each plant.

Wait to add new, less-hardy water garden plants until all danger of frost has passed.

3

Prime the Pump

Water garden pumps (the kind that power waterfalls and fountains) can be stubborn to restart sometimes in the spring after a winter in storage. Test the pump before taking out to the water feature. If it doesn't work and the impeller is not spinning, use a screwdriver or similar advice to nudge the impeller in the right direction. This should prompt it to start spinning, by reintroducing lubrication between the seals and pump.

Other Spring Water Gardening Tips and Techniques

Spring Cleanup in Warm-Climate Areas

Water features in the warmer climates of the country can be treated a little differently in spring. They probably can support bacterial activity year-round, and so may not require a full pond-cleanout. However, they may benefit from a partial cleanout. Spray and clean the filter mats and biomedia or lava rocks. Then do a 20 percent water change.

Give Fish a Boost

Transferring fish out of a pond is very stressful to them. You can ease their stress by using a product called Stress Coat, which will minimize scale damage. Also take the opportunity to examine them up close for any parasites or disease problems. There are several products available online or through fish and water garden speciality stores to treat these.

Keep the holding container in the shade so the water doesn't overheat. And if you must keep fish in a holding container for more than a few hours, add an air pump so oxygen isn't depleted, which would leave the fish gasping and further stressed. You may want to cover the container with a screen or similar material to keep fish from jumping out of the container.

Keep an Eye Out for Other Critters

As you drain the pond, keep an eye out for tadpoles, tiny fish (called fry), and snails in the bottom several inches of water. You may want to keep these to return to the pond.

Save Those Nutrients!

The muck at the bottom makes a great addition to your compost pile. It's rich in nitrogen from fish waste and other decomposed materials. The pond water itself is also rich in nutrients. As much as it is practical and as much as it doesn't flood or blast plants, it's ideal to pump pond water onto beds and borders.

Seasonal Maintenance: Summer Care

Warmer temperatures mean your water garden is more active, so stay on top of small chores before they become big chores.

Periodically review this list to make sure you're keeping up with summertime chores in your water garden. You'll prevent little problems from becoming big ones.

- As needed, step up the cleaning of mechanical filters. Warmer weather can mean more particles to filter out.
- Expect an algae bloom about two to three weeks after cleaning your pond or once the water reaches warmer temperatures. If it doesn't clear up on its own in a week or two, make sure you're doing everything you can to keep your pond balanced (see pages 16–17), or use an algaecide.
- In mid- to late summer, as needed and if desired, divide marginal plants that are severely potbound.
- If you have newly hatched fish, make sure they have protection from larger fish or other predators that may eat them. Mature submerged plants are ideal for them to hide in.
- As temperatures rise, evaporation increases. Top off the pond regularly, but never add more than 10 percent fresh water at a time or you may kill fish.
- Keep yellowed, damaged, or dead foliage trimmed off water garden plants.
- Fertilize water lilies and other heavy feeders regularly with an aquatic plant fertilizer.
- In summer, with plants and insect populations at their peak, fish may get their nourishment elsewhere. Never feed them more than what they can devour completely in 5 minutes or the food decomposes and fouls the water.
- In late summer, if floating plants have covered more of the pond surface than you desire, pull them up and discard.

As summer temperatures rise, water evaporates from your water feature more quickly. Top it off from your garden hose more often, never adding more than 10 percent water.

Seasonal Maintenance: Fall Care

Fall water garden maintenance is all about coping with autumn leaves.

In addition to leaves falling upon your lawn and garden, leaves will also fall into your water feature. Make sure to stay ahead of the leaf fall, preferably every day.

- Skim or rake out leaves from your pond daily or they will break down and encourage algae growth and other problems in the pond. If you have lots of leaves, consider installing a net over the pond or a portion of the pond to catch them.
- If you need to do an overall cleanout of the pond, and plan on keeping it running over the winter, fall is a good time. Fish are strong after summer, and cooler water temperatures keep them more sedate and less likely to be stressed by moving them to clean the pond.
- Determine how you will care for your fish and plants for winter. Stock up, as needed, on grow lights, a de-icer, an oxygen pump, aquarium supplies, and more.

- Keep track of water temperatures (use a specially made water garden thermometer). When temperatures get down to 55° to 50°F, it's time to start preparing your water garden for winter. (See the next page.)

A primary chore of autumn is to net out leaves from your water feature.

A Pump to Clean Out Your Water Garden

From time to time, you'll need to empty or nearly empty your water feature to perform routine cleanings, improvements, or repairs. If the feature is small—less than 100 gallons—you can probably get away with simply bailing the water.

But with larger water gardens, you'll need a pump. Water garden suppliers make special clean-out pumps specifically for this purpose. You can also use a submersible utility pump, used for many other purposes around the house and in construction. These are sometimes loosely referred to as sump pumps, though these more technically are usually what are used in basements to keep them dry.

Seasonal Maintenance: Winter Care

*In mild winter areas with little frost, winter care is minimal. In colder regions,
you'll have to take a few hours to prepare your water feature for winter's worst.*

- Remove any leaves and large bits of debris. A net is helpful for this.
- Trim dead, dying, or excess foliage from plants you plan to overwinter in the pond. Cut back hardy water lilies just above the base. Cut back submerged plants to about 3 inches. Cut marginal plants and hardy water lilies (the only kind that will overwinter) to about 6 inches. Hollow-stemmed marginals, however, should have foliage above the surface or they'll rot.
- It's a good idea to add cold-water bacteria. Made especially for the winter pond that gets below 50° degrees, these bacteria help maintain water clarity and dramatically reduce spring cleanup.
- Leaving your pond running? Water gardens sometimes are at their most stunning in winter, surrounded by snow and ice. If you keep your water feature running, still be sure that the pond is topped off as needed. Also, keep an eye on ice formations so they don't create dams that can force water out of a stream or waterfall.
- Remove the pump from your pond and store it indoors where temperatures don't get below 60°F. Rinse it and store it in a bucket of clean water so the seals don't dry out. Protection from the cold lengthens the life of your pump.
- Drain the water out of pipes and tubing, as much as is practical. This prevents standing water from freezing and expanding, potentially causing cracks and leaks.
- Remove and clean the filter media by spraying with a hose. Store them alongside the pump in a warm spot.
- For information on how to overwinter fish in your area, seek advice from the fish seller.

A de-icer is one option for making your pond suitable for overwintering fish and plants.

Sometimes water gardens can be as lovely in snow as they are at the height of summer.

Water Garden Troubleshooting

Check out these common water garden problems and their solutions.

Problem
Cloudy, green, or otherwise discolored water

Solution
With all water problems, the first thing to consider is if your pond's ecosystem is in balance (see pages 16–17). If all elements seem to be in place, use these indicators to help diagnose the problem:

- **Greenish** water is nearly always a sign of excessive floating algae. An algaecide often will clear up the problem.

- If the water is **reddish brown**, the culprit might be silt or decomposing leaves and debris. Put your hand in the bottom of the pond. If it is muddy and silty, empty and clean the pond if possible (see page 157) and vacuum or bail out silt. If you suspect leaf debris as the culprit, check and clean filters often. Or consider a carbon pond additive. Follow all label directions exactly. You may want to repeat the treatment in two weeks.

- If the water is **blackish**, that's an indicator of extensive pollution from too much organic matter. Empty and refill the pond (see page 157). Make sure you don't have too many fish (see page 72) and that your filtration systems are adequate (see page 58).

- If the water is **whitish**, that's an indicator of bacterial bloom. This problem usually goes away in a couple of weeks.

- If water is **red**, that's a sign of high iron content. Increase aeration with a larger pump/fountain or by adding a waterfall feature.

- If water **smells bad**, in a water feature with fish or plants, it's likely the aeration and filtration system is not adequate or isn't working. If you have filters, make sure they're being rinsed regularly so they can work at full capacity. Consider adding an additional filter (see page 58) to better clarify the water.

  If water smells bad in a fountain or small feature without plants or fish, simply empty the feature, rinse it out, and start with fresh water. Consider adding a slight amount (as in a few drops to a few teaspoons) of chlorine bleach.

- Also, **for all water quality problems**, check out the array of water conditioners and additives available. Some serve as a flocculent, a treatment that clears cloudy water in just a few hours by physically causing particulates in the water to clump together so the filter can filter them out.

  Others contain beneficial bacteria, which consume excess nutrients and break down decaying debris, sludge, or odors. These can be used weekly, if needed.

Problem

String algae is excessive

Solution

- See page 144.

Problem

The GFCI outlet keeps tripping

Solution

- A GFCI tripping more than once or twice every few months is not only annoying, but in winter conditions it could result in a frozen solid pond.
- Make sure moisture isn't getting into the outlet box. Then test each electrical device connected to see if you can determine which is tripping the outlet. Otherwise, have a certified electrician check out the problem.

Problem

After construction, the pond isn't level

Solution

- Continually checking level as you build is the best way to prevent this, of course. But if you've built your feature and it's uneven, the easiest solution is to add more stones, river rock, pea gravel, or other materials to disguise the problem.

  If that's not an option or doesn't work, you'll simply need to remove the edging in the problem area and add to or dig it out to correct the problem.

Problem

Fish occasionally die

Solution

- Pond fish will occasionally die for unknown reasons. And some weaker ones simply don't make it through tough winters. But you shouldn't be losing more than 1 fish in 10 in a year.
- To remedy the problem, make sure you don't have too many fish (see page 72). Overcrowding contributes to more deaths.
- Examine fish closely for signs of the problem. Net the fish into a bucket or wading pool. Examine them closely for signs of disease or external parasites. Various products are available to treat these problems, or you may need to start over and restock.

Problem

Fish are gasping at the surface

Solution

- This is an emergency situation because the water doesn't contain enough oxygen. You can take a hose and forcefully spray water into the feature to add oxygen—just don't add more than 10 percent.
- Make sure the pump is functioning properly. Add some type of aeration to your feature, such as an underwater pump, if you don't have one already.

Problem

Plants don't thrive; they're stunted or leaves keep turning yellow

Solution

- Plants as they grow and mature, over time, will inevitably lose some leaves to natural processes. Trim these off.
- If yellowing leaves account for more than 5 percent of the overall plant, reevaluate how much sun it is getting. Most water garden plants need 6 to 8 hours of full, direct sun a day. Also make sure the plant is suitable for a water garden—it may not like aquatic conditions.
- Consider fertilizing the plant with a special aquatic plant fertilizer tablet.

Problem

A stream or waterfall floods when the pump stops

Solution

- There is not enough capacity in any pond at the foot of the feature. The pond, along with any header pools or other pools along the stream or waterfall, should be designed hold all the water of the feature if the pump stops.
- The only way to remedy this is to expand or build a reservoir pool at the base.

Problem

A filter constantly clogs

Solution

- All filters need to be periodically cleaned. With a mechanical filter, this could be daily. If feel you are cleaning out your filter more than you should, make sure your filter is large enough for your feature (see page 58). Also consider adding a second filter.

How to Find and Repair a Leak

Do you have a leak or is it evaporation? And if you do have a leak,
how in the heck do you find it and fix it?

Is It Just Evaporation?

Ponds can easily lose 1 to 1½ inches of water a week through evaporation and in some areas in some conditions, that can be as much as 3 inches.

One way to determine if it's a leak or evaporation is to set a bucket out near the pond. Note the water level. If the bucket's level drops to a level similar to what your pond is doing, you know it's just evaporation.

Also, splashing waterfalls and other splashing elements allow water to evaporate at a rate higher than what you might expect.

Locating a Leak

Fixing a leak is easy. Finding a leak can be difficult.

One way to locate a leak is to turn off the waterfall or pump and allow the water to drop until it does not appear to be dropping anymore. That will be the level where the leak is located. Search around the perimeter to see if you can find the leak.

If the water doesn't drop with those off, the leak is likely not in the pond but somewhere in the plumbing, filters, stream, or waterfall. More often than not, a leak is the result of water "sneaking" over the edge of the liner. Investigate the perimeter for wet spots and raise the edge of the pond and/or relocate rocks and gravel so the water doesn't continue to leak out.

If that doesn't work, remove any rocks around the entire perimeter at the level where

the water stopped. You can then carefully check for some sort of puncture, or hole in the liner.

As a last resort, you can call in a pond or water garden professional to diagnose and locate the leak.

1

Drain the feature to expose the leak. You may need to remove fish and plants first to do this.

2

Clean the area with water and then denatured alcohol or an adhesive primer. Patch the leak, extending the patch 2 to 4 inches beyond the leak.

3

Apply silicone sealant over the repaired area and allow it to dry. Refill the pond, treat with water conditioners as necessary, and replace fish and plants.

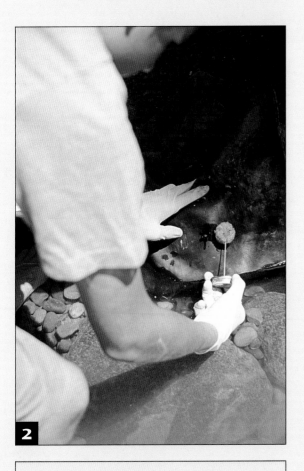

Tools and Supplies

- Fish net
- Buckets
- Clean-out pump or submersible utility pump
- Liner repair kit
- Denatured alcohol or adhesive primer
- Aquarium-grade silicone sealant

Resources

WEBSITES

The amount of information on the Internet on water gardening is nothing short of astounding. But seek out the best, most reliable information. There's a lot of not-very-good information out there too. These are a few of the largest and best sites.

Aquascape

www.aquascapeinc.com

Aquascape, which contributed significantly to this book, is an industry leader in educating professionals and do-it-yourselfers alike. It has a wonderful website loaded with current, highly reliable information and how-to information. Its strength is technical information with excellent explanatory illustrations. It also offers a contractor locator and sells a wide range of water gardening tools, supplies, and accessories. It has several excellent downloadable design and how-to booklets, large and small.

USDA Cooperative Extension Service

http://www.csrees.usda.gov/extension

The USDA's Cooperative Extension service is legendary, and for good reason. It is university-based and nonprofit, providing an unbiased source of horticultural information. There is a horticulture extension service in every state and most counties. Most have garden phone hotlines.

The Extension Service's strength is water garden and bog plant recommendations for your area, though increasingly the USDA horticulture extension is providing more information on water gardening overall.

Lilypons

http://www.lilypons.com

Lilypons has been one of the best-known sources for water garden plants for decades. It also carries tools, supplies, and water gardening accessories.

PLANT & FISH ASSOCIATIONS

Associated Koi Clubs of America

P.O. Box 10879, Costa Mesa, CA 92627

www.akca.org

Aquatic Gardeners Association

P.O. Box 51536, Denton, TX 76206

membership@aquaticgardeners.org

www.aquatic-gardeners.org

The Goldfish Society of America

P.O. Box 551373, Fort Lauderdale, FL 33355

info@goldfishsociety.org

www.goldfishsociety.org

International Waterlily and Water Gardening Society

P.O. Box 546, Greenville, VA 24440

540-337-4507

info@iwgs.org

http://iwgs.org

Local water garden clubs and associations are especially useful, organizing tours and sharing highly localized water gardening information. For a fairly complete listing by state, go to http://www.watergardenersinternational.org/clubs/main.html

SOURCES

There are many sources for distinctive water gardening products and supplies.
This list is a sampling of some of them.

Aquascapes — www.aquascapeinc.com

Alpine Corporation — www.alpine4u.com

BluWorld HoMelements — www.bluworldusa.com/

Bond Manufacturing — www.bondmfg.com

Campania International — www.campaniainternational.com/

Garden Fountains — www.garden-fountains.com

Lowe's Home Improvement — www.lowes.com

Simply Fountains — www.simplyfountains.com/

Smartpond — www.smart-pond.com

The Home Depot — www.homedepot.com/

Glossary

Ammonia: A byproduct of nitrogen; it's a gaseous compound that has a pungent smell and taste.

Algae: Tiny plant-like organisms that grow in water. Certain amounts of algae are beneficial. It can be floating, grow in long ropes, or form a green film on solid surfaces.

Biofalls: A term sometimes used to describe a preformed rigid liner waterfall unit. Often contains a biological filter (usually plastic media balls or stones in a mesh bag).

Biological filter/biofilter: Any filter that uses beneficial bacterial to convert toxic chemicals in the water (usually ammonia from fish waste) into benign substances. There are many different designs using many different bacteria and materials.

Bog garden: An area for planting garden plants that like extremely wet soil—either very damp or with standing water. Often created by putting a liner in a shallow depression in the ground and filling with soil and planting.

Character stone: Distinctive stones, usually among the largest in a water feature, to add character and interest.

Chloramine: A chemical added by cities and other organizations to water supplies in order to kill organisms that might harm humans. However, chloramine is harmful to some fish and therefore must be removed with a special liquid treatment before fish are added.

Circuit breaker: An automatic switch that cuts electrical power if a short circuit or a power overload exceeds the preset safety level.

Dormant: In a condition of biological rest or inactivity characterized by a halt in growth, development, and many metabolic processes.

Ecosystem: An ecological community, working together in harmony.

Filamentous algae: Also known as string algae. A long, ropey kind of algae that clings to liners, rocks, and especially to waterfalls.

Flexible liner: Any plastic or rubber liner made for water gardens. Usually sold precut or by the foot off rolls.

Flow adjuster: A valve that is adjustable and controls the flow of water. It can be a dial-like mechanism built into a pump. Or you can attach a gate or ball valve to a pump to control the output.

Foundation stone(s): Supports the spill stone, usually along the front of the waterfall unit.

Gate stone: Usually located on either side of a waterfall and stream to help channel water over the spill stone and downward.

GFCI or GFI: A type of power outlet that automatically shuts off power when it detects a problem with the circuit, thus preventing shock.

Hardy, cold-hardy: Refers to how well a fish or plant tolerates or survives cold, especially in terms of whether it will last through winter conditions, dependent on the region.

Head: The pressure that must be generated by pump to run a waterfall, fountain, or other pond component. The pump must be capable of lifting the required volume of water to a certain head or height.

Header pool: The pool at the top of a stream or waterfall. Sometimes incorrectly used to refer to a pool that is part of a stream water feature.

Invasive: A plant that spreads far beyond its planned site and is difficult to remove or control.

Landscape fabric: A black plastic-like nonwoven fabric that allows water and air to pass through but blocks weed growth.

Manifold: Pipe, tubing, or other device that diverts water to multiple directions

Marginal plant: In nature, a plant that grows in shallow water at the edge (the margins) of a pond. In manmade features, a marginal plant is any plant grown in a few to several inches of water, usually in pots set on shallow shelves or ledges along the edge of the feature.

Mechanical filter: A filter that removes larger debris, such as leaves, grit, or larger clumps of algae through mechanical means, that is, through simple devices such as meshes or filters.

Nitrites: A compound that is a byproduct of nitrogen that is harmful to fish at even very low levels.

Organic: Any carbon-based form of life, dead or alive.

pH: A measure of acidity or alkalinity on a 14-point scale

Prefilter: A device used with submersible pumps to strain large debris to prevent it from getting caught in the pump. Many different designs. Often used with other filters.

Pre-formed liner: The same as a rigid liner.

PVC: Short for polyvinyl chloride—the heavy-duty plastic material used to make white, black, and other plastic-like pipes.

Rigid liner: A pre-formed liner made of molded plastic or fiberglass. It's available in many different shapes.

Skimmer: A filter designed to "skim" surface debris by allowing just the top surface of the water to flow into the skimmer unit.

Spill stone: A flat stone that water can run over as part of a waterfall.

Submerged plant: A plant that lives completely under the water. It releases oxygen into the water as well as absorbs minerals and carbon dioxide, thus helping to starve the algae and promote a balanced aquatic environment. In addition, submerged plants provide food and shelter for fish.

Transformer: A device for reducing or increasing the voltage of electric current. Used with low-voltage system to reduce the voltage from a regular household current to lower current.

Underlayment: A layer of material installed between the ground and pond liner to prevent punctures from rough or rocky ground.

UV clarifier: A filter that uses ultraviolet light to kill suspended algae and ensure clear pond water. Water flows into the casing that contains the bulb, is exposed to the light, and flows back out again.

Water feature: Any pool, pond, fountain, stream, waterfall, or other water-containing structure.

Water garden: Used generally (and incorrectly) to describe many different water features, but technically refers to one that contains plants.

Weir: Traditionally a low dam built across a stream to raise its level or divert its flow. In water gardening, this word sometimes refers to the deep, rigid liner container with a pre-formed lip used to create waterfalls.

Zones, U.S.D.A. Refers to the areas of North America labeled according to average winter lows by the U.S. Department of Agriculture for the purpose of determining which plants are winter hardy to which regions.

Conversions

Metric Equivalent

Inches (in.)	1/64	1/32	1/25	1/16	1/8	1/4	3/8	2/5	1/2	5/8	3/4	7/8	1	2	3	4	5	6	7	8	9	10	11	12	36	39.4
Feet (ft.)																								1	3	3 1/12
Yards (yd.)																									1	1 1/12
Millimeters (mm)	0.40	0.79	1	1.59	3.18	6.35	9.53	10	12.7	15.9	19.1	22.2	25.4	50.8	76.2	101.6	127	152	178	203	229	254	279	305	914	1,000
Centimeters (cm)							0.95	1	1.27	1.59	1.91	2.22	2.54	5.08	7.62	10.16	12.7	15.2	17.8	20.3	22.9	25.4	27.9	30.5	91.4	100
Meters (m)																								.30	.91	1.00

Converting Measurements

TO CONVERT:	TO:	MULTIPLY BY:
Inches	Millimeters	25.4
Inches	Centimeters	2.54
Feet	Meters	0.305
Yards	Meters	0.914
Miles	Kilometers	1.609
Square inches	Square centimeters	6.45
Square feet	Square meters	0.093
Square yards	Square meters	0.836
Cubic inches	Cubic centimeters	16.4
Cubic feet	Cubic meters	0.0283
Cubic yards	Cubic meters	0.765
Pints (U.S.)	Liters	0.473 (Imp. 0.568)
Quarts (U.S.)	Liters	0.946 (Imp. 1.136)
Gallons (U.S.)	Liters	3.785 (Imp. 4.546)
Ounces	Grams	28.4
Pounds	Kilograms	0.454
Tons	Metric tons	0.907

TO CONVERT:	TO:	MULTIPLY BY:
Millimeters	Inches	0.039
Centimeters	Inches	0.394
Meters	Feet	3.28
Meters	Yards	1.09
Kilometers	Miles	0.621
Square centimeters	Square inches	0.155
Square meters	Square feet	10.8
Square meters	Square yards	1.2
Cubic centimeters	Cubic inches	0.061
Cubic meters	Cubic feet	35.3
Cubic meters	Cubic yards	1.31
Liters	Pints (U.S.)	2.114 (Imp. 1.76)
Liters	Quarts (U.S.)	1.057 (Imp. 0.88)
Liters	Gallons (U.S.)	0.264 (Imp. 0.22)
Grams	Ounces	0.035
Kilograms	Pounds	2.2
Metric tons	Tons	1.1

Converting Temperatures

Convert degrees Fahrenheit (F) to degrees Celsius (C) by following this simple formula: Subtract 32 from the Fahrenheit temperature reading. Then mulitply that number by $\frac{5}{9}$. For example, 77°F - 32 = 45. 45 × $\frac{5}{9}$ = 25°C.

To convert degrees Celsius to degrees Fahrenheit, multiply the Celsius temperature reading by $\frac{9}{5}$, then add 32. For example, 25°C × $\frac{9}{5}$ = 45. 45 + 32 = 77°F.

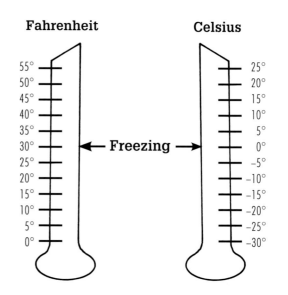

Fahrenheit | Celsius

← Freezing →

Index

Meet Veronica Lorson Fowler

Veronica Lorson Fowler is the author of numerous garden books, including two on water gardening. She is a former newspaper garden columnist and was a garden editor at Better Homes and Gardens Special Interest Publications. Her writing has been published in *Better Homes and Gardens, Horticulture, Country Home,* and many other home and garden magazines. She is the co-creator of *The Iowa Gardener* website and e-newsletter (www.theiowagardener. com). There Veronica shares nifty tips and tricks relevant to Iowa's locale, updates from Iowa experts on weather trends and warnings, updates on pest and disease issues affecting Iowans, features of the newest and best plants for an Iowa garden, and special articles about upcoming garden shows, plant sales, horticultural events, festivals, and tours.

A Kansas farm girl who grew up gardening, she now lives in Ames, Iowa, where she tends her own extensive landscape, which includes one water garden. She describes herself as a "complete garden geek" who raised her three children amid a sometimes messy but always very varied garden.